THE WAY OF SIMPLICITY

THE WAY OF SIMPLICITY

The Cistercian Tradition

ESTHER DE WAAL

SERIES EDITOR:
Philip Sheldrake

ORBIS BOOKS

Maryknoll, New York 10545

The Catholic Foreign Mission Society of America (Maryknoll) recruits and trains people for overseas missionary service. Through Orbis Books, Maryknoll aims to foster the international dialogue that is essential to mission. The books published, however, reflect the opinions of their authors and are not meant to represent the official position of the society.

First published in 1998 by
Darton, Longman and Todd Ltd.
1 Spencer Court
140–142 Wandsworth High Street
London SW18 4JJ
Great Britain

Published in the USA in 1998 by
Orbis Books
P.O. Box 308
Maryknoll, New York 10545–0308
U.S.A.

ISBN 1–57075–195–1

Designed by Sandie Boccacci
Phototypeset in 10/13¼pt New Century Schoolbook
by Intype London Ltd
Printed and bound in Great Britain by
Redwood Books, Trowbridge, Wiltshire

Library of Congress Cataloging-in-Publication Data

De Waal, Esther.
    The way of simplicity : the Cistercian tradition / Esther De Waal.
      p.   cm.—(Traditions of Christian spirituality)
    Includes bibliographical references and index.
    ISBN 1–57075–195–1 (pbk.)
    1. Cistercians—Spiritual life.   I. Title.   II. Series.
  BX3403.   1998
  255'.12—dc21   98–18341
                                                                      CIP

For Bethany

CONTENTS

PREFACE TO THE SERIES

Nowadays, in the western world, there is a widespread hunger for spirituality in all its forms. This is not confined to traditional religious people let alone to regular churchgoers. The desire for resources to sustain the spiritual quest has led many people to seek wisdom in unfamiliar places. Some have turned to cultures other than their own. The fascination with Native American or Aboriginal Australian spiritualities is a case in point. Other people have been attracted by the religions of India and Tibet or the Jewish Kabbalah and Sufi mysticism. One problem is that, in comparison to other religions, Christianity is not always associated in people's minds with 'spirituality'. The exceptions are a few figures from the past who have achieved almost cult status such as Hildegard of Bingen or Meister Eckhart. This is a great pity for Christianity East and West over two thousand years has given birth to an immense range of spiritual wisdom. Many traditions continue to be active today. Others that were forgotten are being rediscovered and reinterpreted.

It is a long time since an extended series of introductions to Christian spiritual traditions has been available in English. Given the present climate, it is an opportune moment for a new series which will help more people to be aware of the great spiritual riches available within the Christian tradition.

The overall purpose of the series is to make selected spiritual traditions available to a contemporary readership. The books seek to provide accurate and balanced historical and thematic treatments of their subjects. The authors are also conscious of the need to make connections with contemporary experience and values without being artificial or reducing a tradition to one dimension. The authors are well-versed in reliable scholarship about the traditions they describe. However, their intention is that the books should be fresh in style and accessible to the general reader.

One problem that such a series inevitably faces is the word 'spirituality'. For example, it is increasingly used beyond religious circles and does not necessarily imply a faith tradition. Again, it could mean substantially different things for a Christian and a Buddhist. Within Christianity itself, the word in its modern sense is relatively recent. The reality that it stands for differs subtly in the different contexts of time and place. Historically, 'spirituality' covers a breadth of human experience and a wide range of values and practices.

No single definition of 'spirituality' has been imposed on the authors in this series. Yet, despite the breadth of the series there is a sense of a common core in the writers themselves and in the traditions they describe. All Christian spiritual traditions have their source in three things. First, while drawing on ordinary experience and even religious insights from elsewhere, Christian spiritualities are rooted in the scriptures and particularly in the gospels. Second, spiritual traditions are not derived from abstract theory but from attempts to live out gospel values in a positive yet critical way within specific historical and cultural contexts. Third, the experiences and insights of individuals and groups are not isolated but are related to the wider Christian tradition of beliefs, practices and community life. From a Christian perspective, spirituality is not just concerned with prayer or even with narrowly religious activities. It concerns the whole of human life, viewed in terms of a conscious relationship with God, in Jesus Christ, through the indwelling of the Holy Spirit and within a community of believers.

The series as a whole includes traditions that probably would not have appeared twenty years ago. The authors themselves have been encouraged to challenge, where appropriate, inaccurate assumptions about their particular tradition. While conscious of their own biases, authors have nonetheless sought to correct the imbalances of the past. Previous understandings of what is mainstream or 'orthodox' sometimes need to be questioned. People or practices that became marginal demand to be re-examined. Studies of spirituality in the past frequently underestimated or ignored the role of women. Sometimes the treatments of spiritual traditions were culturally one-sided because they were written from an uncritical western European or North Atlantic perspective.

However, any series is necessarily selective. It cannot hope to do full justice to the extraordinary variety of Christian spiritual traditions. The principles of selection are inevitably open to question. I hope that an appropriate balance has been maintained between a sense of the likely readership on the one hand and the dangers of narrowness on the other. In the end, choices had to be made and the result is inevitably weighted in favour of traditions that have achieved 'classic' status or which seem to capture the contemporary imagination. Within these limits, I trust that the series will offer a reasonably balanced account of what the Christian spiritual tradition has to offer.

As editor of the series I would like to thank all the authors who agreed to contribute and for the stimulating conversations and correspondence that sometimes resulted. I am especially grateful for the high quality of their work which made my task so much easier. Editing such a series is a complex undertaking. I have worked closely throughout with Morag Reeve of Darton, Longman & Todd and Robert Ellsberg of Orbis Books. I am immensely grateful to them for their friendly support and judicious advice. Without them this series would never have come together.

PHILIP SHELDRAKE
Sarum College, Salisbury

INTRODUCTION

My encounter with the early Cistercian fathers and mothers, and with present day Cistercian writing, has been an exciting experience, opening new doors, taking me into areas of thought and writing that I have found energising and stimulating, and not least, of practical help in my daily life. The guide in my Christian discipleship has for many years now been St Benedict, and I have found his Rule both encouraging and challenging, wise, gentle and tough. Now, as I discover the Cistercians of the twelfth century, it is as though I am being helped to come to the Rule of St Benedict afresh. In their lives and writings I have been given new and invigorating insights, and have been led more deeply into an understanding of contemplative prayer and mystical union with God. Their one desire was simply to follow the Rule more closely, to return to what they believed to be its original inspiration. Inevitably they brought a new approach, a different emphasis which reflected their changed world, not least minds formed by the new learning of the twelfth-century renaissance. I have been reading not only works of men like St Bernard of Clairvaux or St Aelred of Rievaulx but also men much less well known, like Gilbert of Hoyland and John of Forde, who wrote with remarkable gifts of wisdom and poetic expression. These men have become my 'Fathers and friends' – to use a phrase of Thomas Merton, the American Cistercian monk of our own day who wrote so much about his own monastic life and the Cistercian commitment which shaped it. I shall be quoting him frequently, together with other contemporary Cistercian monks and nuns who remind us of the flourishing spiritual and intellectual life of the order throughout the world today.

I first came to know St Benedict through the experience of living for ten years in Canterbury, under the shadow of a great Benedictine monastic church and surrounded by its ruins. Once again, by God's amazing sense of timing, I have come to live only a few miles from a Cistercian abbey. So although I have read as widely as I could it is not words alone that have gone into the writing of this book. A sense of place which this building and its surroundings brought has also made an important contribution. Dore Abbey, however, is unique amongst the English medieval Cistercian abbeys – it is a living place of worship. It was founded on 25 April 1147, in the lifetime of St Bernard, by a small group of monks from Morimond in France. At the Reformation it came into the hands of a local family, and in the early seventeenth century its owner Lord Scudamore, a good friend of Archbishop William Laud, the Catholic-minded Archbishop of Canterbury, rededicated the chancel and restored the altar, added new windows and woodwork. The choir of the medieval abbey was thus restored as an Anglican parish church, and Abbey Dore stands as a testimony to the continuity of past and present.

Whenever I can, I like to approach it by walking across the fields, over a small stream and the monks' conduit; I like to sit and read and pray in the small square orchard, the site of the cloisters; when I go into the church itself and sit inside I watch the faces of visitors as they come in through its door and are met by the immensity of its space and silence. From each of these experiences I learn something that is more than words alone could bring. The way in which it is so clearly set in the surrounding countryside (the used machinery from the nearby farm standing in the fields is very natural) tells me about a spirituality firmly earthed in the land. The cloisters present the question: what other complex of buildings puts emptiness at its heart? I find that I am asking myself what kind of life revolves around a centre which is open and uncluttered. When I go into the church itself I am struck every time by the pared down beauty of the simplicity of the architecture. The enormous height and the clear lines have a calming effect which is almost palpable. But above all it is as though the actual building throws one back on oneself and on God.

I am grateful for this since the weight of words is terrifying. I know enough of Cistercian scholarship to be aware of the continuing flow of new books, of the critical editions of the Cistercian fathers and mothers, and the important articles contained in the volumes of *Cistercian Studies Quarterly*, and other learned periodicals, of conferences such as the annual gathering of monastic scholars at Kalamazoo. This is not an academic study, although I have tried to be true throughout to the texts themselves, since they are such incomparable writing. I have included so much original material for that reason, and have often set it out as though it were in the form of a prose-poem, a liberty I hope that both the Cistercian fathers and their editors will forgive, but I felt that this would encourage more slow and prayerful reading. The monastic way of *lectio divina*, by which one reads and ponders, weighing lines and phrases in the heart and mind, slow prayer-filled reading which takes time, is an art that I feel we need in an age when we are expected to read so much and at such speed. This means, in the words of St Benedict, attending 'with the ear of the heart'.

For I have not studied the Cistercian tradition in order to acquire information as much as wisdom and practical help. As I read, the most important question was always what difference was this going to make in my own life? In the way in which I come to know God? In the way in which I pray? In short, am I going to be changed by what I find? It is good to be reminded by Fr Basil Pennington, a contemporary Cistercian, that one of the reasons why we have so much Cistercian material today is that their writings were constantly copied and widely diffused throughout the Middle Ages amongst literate people. In his own work on St Bernard and his disciples his hope is that his readers will find them 'most loving and

God-filled Fathers', who will open out new vistas of life, and new depths of joy.[1]

Thomas Merton has probably done more than anyone else by his writings to make the monastic life accessible and intelligible to ordinary lay people today. His close friend and secretary Br Patrick Hart has said that he studied early Cistercian texts 'with a view to gaining insights into his own life'. Dom Jean Leclercq, one of the greatest monastic scholars of our day, tells us that when he visited Merton's monastery of Gethsemani and was shown the edition of St Bernard that Merton had used, his careful reading was immediately manifest in the marginal notes, glosses and references to complementary texts.[2] Yet having so carefully assimilated it, he wrote not as a historian but as a witness to a living tradition, with the result that his treatment is contemplative, the fruit of his own meditated reading. But then the secret of the man whom he was studying is that St Bernard too was writing out of his own experience. He himself insists 'I am telling you of what I have myself experienced'.

These Cistercian men and women show us the way, and share the journey, pointing us towards the mystery of Christ and the action of grace within our own lives. Jean Leclercq has warned against 'Bernardology', and there is perhaps an even greater need for caution in the case of Thomas Merton who is rapidly becoming virtually a cult figure as an increasing flood of books, theses and articles about him are published every year. Jean Leclercq imagines St Bernard's quiet smile as he says 'My secret is mine'. I take that as a vital keynote for this book, reminding us that we can never hope to possess, or even understand fully. Here we are given another source of help on our Christian journey, one which each of us has the opportunity to take into our lives in whatever God-given way is appropriate for the point at which we find ourselves on that journey.

I have at intervals incorporated a few words of the original Latin, a short phrase – though always accompanied by a translation! This is partly for the sheer pleasure of the words themselves, the alliteration which abounds in the Latin text, a balancing of words that is a delight to both ear and mind, but also since I felt that in some incalculable way the words themselves can become a bridge connecting us with the past. It was for this reason that I have also included a long final chapter which is an anthology of extracts of original material which so delighted me when I read them that I wanted others to be able to enjoy them as well. They are mainly taken from sermons, many of them inaccessible to the ordinary reader in learned periodicals or academic texts. I have taken a few sentences and set them out as prose-poems, so that they can be read slowly and prayerfully.

My concern has been throughout with the Cistercian tradition, as it is revealed in its writings. I have not gone into the historical development of the order after describing its origins in the deserts of Cîteaux in 1098 and the emergence of its original charism. There is nothing therefore about the seventeenth century reforms of La Trappe and for the sake of simplification I refer throughout to 'Cistercians' and have not used the word 'Trappist'.

When I was preparing to write this book I found myself trying to snatch time in a busy life of travelling, lecturing, taking retreats and leading pilgrimages. I have therefore some vivid memories of reading Cistercian texts in most unlikely places – on the top of a London bus, while waiting to meet some Canadian pilgrims at Terminal 3 in Heathrow, perched on rocks in Ireland waiting to see if we could get across to Skellig Michael. But when it came to the writing itself I was able to take time to be alone, to stay in one place, and to impose upon myself something of a monastic rhythm of prayer, writing and work on the river bank and in the orchard of this cottage in the Welsh Borders. In some mysterious way praying and writing and manual work seemed to fuse so that everything began to interconnect and to flow from one centre. I was fascinated to find this validated by something that I was reading at the time by May Sarton, describing her own life as a writer in *Plant Dreaming Deep*: 'A day divided between writing in the morning and gardening in the afternoon has a good balance, it is possible to maintain what might be called perfect pitch, total awareness for a good many hours of such a day . . .'[3] It was as though once again I was finding that the monastic understanding expresses something basic to our humanity, a reflection of the way in which we were meant to live fully and creatively.

I have one wish only as I finish this book, to be first published in the year which commemorates the original foundation of Cîteaux in 1098, and that is that it may encourage other lay people like myself to go further in their own exploration into the incomparable riches of this tradition – and that they will discover for themselves the Cistercian fathers and mothers as friends and guides for their Christian journey.

A NOTE ABOUT PRESENTATION

In writing this book I have inevitably relied almost entirely on the scholarship and above all on the translations of others. It seemed quite pointless therefore to give the actual reference to any of these sources, since this would be extremely complicated and would merely end up with this sort of hieroglyphics: *Vita Prima*, ch. XII, n.57–60, *PL* 185.259–60. I have therefore only given the reference to the secondary sources.

When I quote a contemporary Cistercian, such as Michael Casey or Basil Pennington, for the first time, I shall briefly introduce them. But for the twelfth-century monastics or for anyone such as Thomas Merton who is no longer living, I have added a short portrait gallery in the first appendix to the book so that when you first come across Guerric of Igny or Gilbert of Hoyland, for example, you can refer to this section of the book.

Although I have used the terms St Bernard and St Benedict in this introduction, throughout the rest of the book I shall be dropping that appellation in accord with what is now a more common practice.

I faced a problem with language, and decided that, only too aware of accusations of being sexist, I would still have to speak of monk – and man. To say monks and nuns or men and women every time would have been extremely clumsy and infelicitous. There was the added difficulty in any case that most of the time it is a man who is speaking. But I should like to make it clear that almost from the first there have been women in the Cistercian order, that they have always been significant, that we are more and more coming to recognise their contribution. There are nearly two thousand nuns throughout the world today and their scholarship in all areas of the monastic field is most impressive, and not least in showing us medieval women of the stature and originality of Beatrice of Nazareth, whose writings we are only just coming to know.

1. THE BUILDING

In a Cistercian building we find a 'subdued and bare art'.[1]
Here is simplicity, in the use of authentic materials, the careful
blending of light and shade, the emphasis on sobriety of line.
Here there is nothing superfluous that might distract the mind
from God. This austere beauty, without decoration, fancy
sculpture or stained glass, has a calming, almost a purifying
effect, which seems to throw us back on ourselves, and on God.
From the very start in the twelfth century the Cistercians
built their monasteries with one simple purpose – to make
them places of prayer. Whether it is the work of the Middle
Ages, Senanque or Fontenay in France, Rievaulx or Tintern in
Britain, or of the twentieth century, the Abbey of the Genesee
in upstate New York or the recently rebuilt Belgian abbey
Notre-Dame de St Remy in Rochefort, makes little difference.
As Dom André Louf, Abbot of the Abbey of Mont des Cats,
says in *The Cistercian Way*,

> The Cistercian spirit of simplicity is engraved to this day
> on the very stones . . . Beauty and simplicity preserve the
> spirit from distraction and lead it to God. Beauty leads to
> contemplation and is a sort of sacrament of the eternal
> beauty of God.[2]

There is a parallel here with the icon painter who is attempting
to express the inexpressible. By stripping their churches of
everything that was sumptuous they have somehow made
present the transcendence of God.

'Cistercian architecture explains many things about our rule
and our life,' wrote Thomas Merton in *The Sign of Jonas* in

January 1947, six years after he had entered the abbey of
Gethsemani. Since he had spent his early years in Europe, the
son of artist parents brought up in the south of France, he was
in a position to speak of the riches of a church such as that of
Senanque in Provence:

> A church like Senanque is born of prayer and is a prayer.
> Its simplicity and its energy tell us what our prayer should
> be. It simply says what Saint Benedict already told us:
> that we must pray to God 'with all humility and purity of
> devotion . . . not in many words but in purity of heart and
> in the compunction of tears'. The churches of our Fathers
> expressed their humility and their silence. There was
> nothing superfluous about either the office of our Fathers
> or their architecture, nothing useless in their private
> prayer. They did not waste words with God or with men
> and in their buildings they did not waste anything
> either . . . They knew a good building would praise God
> better than a bad one.

At the end of that year he wrote:

> The perfection of twelfth-century Cistercian architecture
> is not to be explained by saying that the Cistercians were
> looking for a new technique. I am not sure that they
> were looking for a new technique at all. They built good
> churches because they were looking for God. And they
> were looking for God in a way that was pure and integral
> enough to make everything they did and everything they
> touched give glory to God.[3]

There is in the Cistercian tradition concern not only for the
natural environment but also for the humanly constructed one.
Their spirituality was after all wholistic – they did not split
matter and spirit, material and spiritual. The actual monastic
buildings provide the framework for a daily life in which, living
according to the Rule, they were expected to show a reverence
and respect not only in the handling of all goods and tools but
also to place and space. As I have come to know their buildings,

essentially functional architecture which reflects the necessities of their daily life, I have also come to see much about the purity, simplicity and strength of that life.

Amongst the abbey churches which were built under the immediate influence of Bernard's own abbey church at Clairvaux and which are still standing, Fontenay is the earliest, although over 150 oratories which adopted a basic plan and elevation are either extant or are known by historical record. 'In all its variety of regional versions and its differences in scale, the Cistercian oratory of St Bernard's generation makes a strong claim upon the modern imagination as a building that moves with chaste directness towards its objective: it is an uncompromising environment of prayer.'[4] It is fascinating to see how the parts relate to one another, and how the proportions are based on a modular construction, using the width of the crossing as a unit. The height of the nave in relation to its width is two to one; the cross-section of the building is a perfect square. The nave, covered with a barrel vault, produces excellent acoustics. The flat chevet at the east end is not only economical but allows a great deal of window space which, together with the windows from the west wall, provides indirect white light. There is no need for clerestory windows since the office to be sung is generally known by heart. Here is the perfectly functional church, all its elements clearly interbalanced.

Reading the visual message of the monastic complex itself I see buildings designed for a life of work, study and prayer, in that balance of body, mind and spirit which Benedict had originally established. Since around the year 800 a standard pattern had been developed with two features which were universal: a large church and a quadrangular cloister. The cloister ran off the north side of the church in countries where the monks sought shade, and the south in Britain where it was important to receive as much warmth as possible, unless as at Dore the lie of the land dictated otherwise. Running off the cloisters were the dormitory and the refectory which served the physical needs of the body: spacious open dormitories, with long rows of simple cots and straw pallets, which was a part of being 'poor with the poor Christ'. The chapter house was the meeting place, where faults would be publicly acknowledged and punished, and where administration and community business took place, such as the election of a new abbot. The scriptorium and library served the needs of the mind, that serious attention to things of the intellect and academic learning that has always been a mark of the Cistercian life. In addition there were other necessary places such as the lavatorium, and the calefactorium, where in winter the monks would find a big fire after the night office and where they could take refuge from the cold during short intervals.

The cloister was not only practical and functional, it was also symbolic. They would pass along this quadrangle, the link-line bringing into relationship the succession of buildings which served their daily needs. None of these is set apart as intrinsically different or superior to any other. Here is a life which is not a succession of alternating superior and inferior activities, but rather a continuous rhythm of equally valid ones. We can look on it in terms of an interplay between stable places and the pathways that link them: an ordering of space which encouraged the sense of unity and cohesion. The cloister walk encloses the garth or garden, where often there would be a cistern or fountain, so that there was a supply of water to keep plants alive – again something which I read as a symbol of the interior place within each of us and the importance of that nurturing flow of living water to keep it green and alive. This is of course a description of the traditional monastery as it would be widely found until about 1950. Since then many modern monasteries are being built all over the world with endless variety – perhaps in campus style, or as a scattered village, or centring on the church like spokes in a wheel.

But always the church remains the pivot of their lives, to which they will return at intervals throughout the day, for it is this which holds together the balanced life, which employs body and mind as well as spirit of this wholistic spirituality. The entire complex is thus the workshop where God's work is done, both the opus Dei, the work of God in prayer and praise, and the work of sleeping and studying, of serving food and eating, and the manual labour by which they earned their living and sustained their common life.

For those who had to be separate from the main complex, there was provision for the sick in the infirmary, and for guests, who would be received in the guesthouse. At slightly further distance lay workshops and farms, and then, that new and distinctive feature of their monastic reform, the numbers of granges widely scattered throughout the surrounding country-side. These granges were in many respects almost like small monasteries, and indeed some were elevated to that status. Each grange consisted of a complex of farm buildings – barns, stables, an oratory and residential accommodation, sur-rounded by a precinct wall or bank. They were lived in by a small community of lay brothers, under the command of one of their number called the *grangiarius* or grange-master. At harvest time the choir monks (making the point that they still lived by the labour of their hands!) might be sent to a grange for several days at a time and dormitories were kept in readi-ness for them there.

Walter Daniel's *Life of Aelred*, written soon after Aelred's death, described how the first monks sited themselves on the banks of the river Rie, a turbulent stream flowing through a broad valley, surrounded by trees. As he writes he waxes lyrical about this landscape of water and trees which is for him nothing less than a 'second Eden':

> High hills surround the valley, encircling it like a crown. With their motley mantle of trees they offer pleasant retreats and ensure the seclusion of the vale, their wooded delights affording the monks a kind of second Eden. Spring waters come tumbling down from the highest rocks to the valley below, and, threading their way down narrow clefts and gullies, they widen out to rivulets and rills, uniting the murmur of their softly purling voices in a sweet concert of harmonious sound. And when the

branches of the lovely trees clash and part with a rhythmical soughing as the leaves flutter gently to the ground, the blissful listener enjoys a wealth of jubilant harmony.[5]

We can only guess what it must have been like for those very earliest Cistercians as they took over the marginal land that was all that was generally available to them, since most of the easily worked agricultural land had already been put under cultivation. But the accounts of nineteenth-century missionary orders in Africa may help to give some idea. Abbot Francis Pfanner was born in Austria in 1825 and began life as a miner before joining the missionary Marianhill Trappist order. When he was in his mid-fifties he went to found a monastery in southern Africa. Setting sail in July 1880 with a group of thirty men they landed at the end of the month in Port Elizabeth and set out from there walking, 'singing and praying like pious troopers'. This joyousness however soon gave way to depression at what they found:

> You could take it all in at a glance. The spot where we stood was raised some feet above the thorny plain and bordered on one side by the perpendicular rock-face of the White River. From this cliff you could see all round over a vast expanse of the surrounding thorny desert.

The site looked desperate but they set about examining plants and rocks, digging for water, testing the quality of the soil. The prior's first report gives a vivid picture:

> Far away on the edge of a steep, rocky slope a brother is busy with a hive of bees. Opposite a brother is hard at it in a half-built smithy with no roof over the fire, forging a ploughshare, while near him a monk is hauling in giant thorns with a horse so that one of the fathers can use them to build a fence round the cattle-pen. A little further off a lay-brother is watering the vine slips he planted a few days ago in the cactus soil. You can see another brother nearby baking bread in a field oven ... Not far away one brother is making a new cart and another a garden-

sprayer of tin-plate, both working in the open air since
there are no workshops . . .

This is a story that could be repeated time and time again –
as also the disppointments and failures that preceded the final
success, which was in this case Marianhill, where mass was
celebrated for the first time on 27 December 1882, feast of St
John the Evangelist. It also began as a canvas monastery, with
offices said in the open air. It was called Marianhill in honour
of the Mother of God and St Anne, the grandmother. On a
return journey with eleven brothers, twelve novices and six
Swiss nuns, who had volunteered to go to Africa (together
with machinery and building materials), Francis Pfanner took
advantage of telling the rest of the passengers about the life
that lay ahead for them:

> I offer them a hard palliasse to sleep on and coarse woven
> clothes to wear. I demand hard manual work, like digging,
> threshing, mowing, washing, chopping wood and scrub-
> bing floors – and all this in the heat, wind, ice and snow.
> I require them all to get up at two o'clock in the
> morning . . . You are right to shake your heads. You cannot
> grasp such things. But in the Christian church it is like
> that, a great garden of wonders with all kinds of flowers;
> there are flowers with different colours and scents. Many
> are hidden and alone, like lilies among thorns . . .[6]

Ten years after its foundation there were over two hundred
and fifty men at Marianhill, a whole world of its own, with
workshops, bakery, photographic studio, guest house, and
school house with dormitories for the children, as well as
the cowsheds, fields, gardens. And so there came about, in the
words of its historian, this 'fertile oasis' in Natal.

The transition from wilderness to paradise was repeated
time and again in not dissimilar ways in the twelfth century.
The names themselves catch this quality of beauty: Clairvaux,
'clear valley' or 'valley of light'; Dore, actually the Welsh for
'water', but thought to mean 'golden', after the French;

Mellifont, 'fountain of honey'; Valuisant, 'shining valley'; Senanque, *sana aqua*, 'clean water'. There is a delightful piece in which an unknown writer who must have been a frequent visitor at Clairvaux describes the co-operation between man and nature in the handling of their water system. It is an extremely romantic account but also illuminating for the way in which it shows their management of the water that played a succession of vital roles in their life.

> Where the orchard ends the garden begins, marked out into rectangles, or, more accurately, divided up by a network of streamlets, for, although the water appears asleep, it is in fact slipping slowly away. Here too a pretty spectacle is afforded to the sick, who can sit on the grassy banks of the clear runnels watching the fish at play in the translucent water, their manoeuvres recalling troops in battle. This water, which serves the dual purpose of feeding the fish and irrigating the vegetables, is supplied by the tireless course of the river Aube, which flows through the many workshops of the abbey. Wherever it passes it evokes a blessing in its wake, proportionate to its good offices; for it does not slip through unscathed or at its leisure, but at the cost of much exertion ...

A winding channel cut by the monks in the middle of the valley sends half its water into the monastery; sluice gates allow it to be harnessed for use in the mill for grinding the grain; the fullers next door to the mill use it where, raising and lowering by turns the heavy pestles (unless you prefer the term mallets, or better still, wooden feet – the expression which seems most suited to the gymnastic occupation of the fullers), it frees these brothers from their drudgery. It then continues on, decanted into a succession of channels, through a series of workshops,

> diligently inquiring where it can be of service and offering its ungrudging help in the work of cooking, sifting, turning, whetting, watering, washing, grinding and softening.

Then finally it carries the waste products away, leaving everything clean in its wake, and

> while Clairvaux renders it thanks for all its blessings it courteously returns the abbot's greetings as it hastens away to pour back into the river the waters siphoned off into the monastery.[7]

There is no doubt about it, Cistercian sites seize the imagination. Those in ruins have always been popular with poets and artists as well as archaeologists and historians, while those which are living are endlessly sought out by writers and above all by photographers.[8]

But there is also the symbolic level. The monastery itself can tell me much about the ordering of my own self. Monastic architecture defines space and provides a structure for a life lived within clearly established boundaries. I am given a vision of relatedness, so that the parts are brought into a harmonious whole. This movement from one centred space to another always returns to the church itself, so that everything flows into and out from the times of prayer. Each element of the person is honoured – body, mind and spirit treated with respect so that each can become an offering to God of the entire self. But it is prayer which holds it together: everything is anchored in prayer, for the church is always the base line, as it were, of the cloisters, the foundation, the point of reference which brings coherence and stability.

But the cloisters, which so often contained an inner garth or garden, bring to the heart of the monastic complex an open space, which becomes the spatial metaphor for interiority, for the cave of the heart, for the innermost self. If the garden is to flourish it must be looked after and cultivated through the differing seasons, and above all it must be watered if it is to flourish. Because of this necessity for the continuing attention that is required there is no escape from hard work, and from remaining in touch with that spring or cistern which was so frequently an integral part of the garden – the spring of the water of the Word with which Cistercians never lost contact.

2. CHARISM

These remarkable men, famed for their religious life, were known as white monks after the colour of their habit, for they were clothed angel-like in undyed sheep's wool, spun and woven from the natural fleece. Thus garbed, when clustered together they look like flocks of gulls, and shine as they walk with the very whiteness of snow.[1]

These flocks of white birds, as Walter Daniel, monk of Rievaulx, so charmingly describes these first Cistercians, descended to colonise the whole of Europe in a way that is almost without parallel.

The *Exordium Parvum*, probably written around 1120, the document which chronicles the start of the order, opens with the ringing declaration: 'We monks of Cîteaux, first founders of this church, inform our successors by this present text through whose agency and in what circumstances the monastery and our way of life came into being . . .'[2] The Cistercians needed to tell their story time and again, for like all reformers throughout the ages, they wanted to explain that the reason why they were leaving the mainstream tradition was to regain what they believed to be a truer and more authentic way of life – in their case life according to the Rule of Benedict. It was therefore literally and symbolically a return to the desert when in 1098 Robert, Abbot of Molesmes, and twenty-one monks

> set out eagerly for a wilderness known as Cîteaux, a locality in the diocese of Chalon where men rarely penetrated and none but wild things lived, so densely covered

was it then with woodland and thorn bush. When the men of God arrived there and realised that the less attractive and accessible the site was to laymen the better it would suit themselves, they began, after felling and clearing the close-growing thickets and bushes, to build a monastery . . .[3]

They made their settlement in a marshy clearing in the woodland south of Dijon in Burgundy in France, calling their first house at Cîteaux the new monastery to distinguish it not only from the mother house but from the rest of the monastic world.[4] Here they experienced the demands of the desert in all its rigours. If we are to understand and appreciate the Cistercian charism fully then the place of the desert, literally and symbolically, is vital. 'Consider the voice of the desert, the blessedness of the desert,' said Guerric of Igny in an Advent sermon; 'the desert will feed you.' And reminding them of the crowds who had followed Jesus into the desert he continued, 'And much more frequently and in an even more wonderful way will he satisfy the needs of all you who have followed him into the desert and whose service is all the more pleasing since your purpose is so much holier'.

For they took seriously what Benedict said in that final chapter of what he so modestly called his 'little rule for beginners', when he told his disciples to read further in Basil, Cassian, the desert fathers. So the model is that of Antony fleeing into the Egyptian desert to live a life of simplicity and austerity, or that of Cassian's teaching on an asceticism that reached almost heroic proportions. Cîteaux was a desert peopled by the ascetics of the twelfth century, and that analogy between monastery and desert has continued to be the Cistercian way, as André Louf explains.

It is in the desert that the soul most often receives its deepest inspiration. It was in the desert that God fashioned his People . . . That is why the monastery is a kind of prophetic place, an anticipation of the world to come, a permanent declaration of a universe remade in

God, a universe whose poles are charity and the praise of
God.[5]

In addition to the physical and spiritual demands those
early days also saw a succession of setbacks. Their first abbot,
obeying a papal injunction to return, took half the brothers
with him. The remaining brothers, first under Abbot Alberic
and then under the Englishman Stephen Harding, who had
been a boy in the cloister at Sherborne, held on in the face of
poverty, austerity and illness. But in the end many sought
them out, wishing to join the new community, amongst them
a man called Bernard who arrived with a large company, of
uncles, brothers, cousins and nephews. This was a turning
point, not only for the immediate community but the whole
order. Within four years, at the age of twenty-five, Bernard
had been appointed abbot of the foundation at Clairvaux, and
within a few years men were thronging in their hundreds, not
only to these earliest abbeys in France, but to new foundations
throughout the whole of Europe.

The extent to which the order owed its phenomenal success
to the personality of Bernard is a perennial question of debate,
and it is very difficult to say how much the expansion of
Cîteaux was due to his presence. David Knowles, himself a
Benedictine monk and well known for his studies of monastic
history, hazards a guess that without him the order would
have remained relatively small, perhaps half its size. The man
was charismatic, a leader, writer, politician, with extraordinary
personal magnetism and spiritual strength in a mix that was
almost irresistible. By the time of his death in 1153 there
were 339 houses, of which Clairvaux, his own foundation from
Cîteaux, had itself founded sixty-eight, from which had sprung
a further ninety-one. The first settlement of white monks in
Britain was in the comparative obscurity of Waverley in Surrey
in 1128. The really significant moment came with the foundation of Rievaulx in 1132 as a daughter house of Cîteaux,
and this was followed a few months later by the exodus of a
band of reformers from the Benedictine abbey of St Mary's in

York to form the nucleus of Fountains. For the next twenty years the growth continued apace and in 1152 there were forty Cistercian houses, mainly in the north of England. In about 1140 Bernard sent a colony to west Wales, which eventually settled in Whitland where once again today there is a Cistercian community of women. Whitland and its daughter house Strata Florida were both wealthy and attracted novices from the ruling families in Wales, and from them further foundations were made in north Wales and in Ireland.

These growing numbers demanded some form of simple, strong organisation to hold them together and Stephen Harding recognised that this was a problem that must be tackled. He was a statesman with a clear mind and even if he did not in fact pen *The Charter of Charity* there is no doubt that it represents his vision for the order. He knew how vital it was to establish a legislative system with a firm chain of authority. There were provisions for a general chapter of all the abbots and a simple system of affiliation and visitation which would bring a thorough system for internal supervision, isolated from external interference and free both from ecclesiastical and secular authority. Sir Richard Southern, a leading medievalist, has called it a masterpiece of medieval planning. In one stroke the Cistercians achieved the first effective international organisation in Europe, more effective even than the papal organisation, since it had narrower aims and a smaller field of operation.[6]

Particularly significant was the freedom they gained by cutting loose from any form of tie or obligation to the feudal society around them. They also cut themselves loose from other accretions which, over the centuries, had grown up around the Benedictine monasteries so that things originally good in themselves had now become shackling or burdensome. Thus they dispensed with the system of child oblates, who came to the monasteries to be educated and spent their early lives in the community; funeral ceremonies for lay patrons disappear; there are no longer relics for public veneration, no pilgrims, no crowds. *A mundalium tumultu mira libertas* – 'liberation from the multiple tensions and conflicts of life in the world'. Merton saw the early Cistercian monasteries as places of order, harmony and peace in marked contrast not only to the world outside but also to the great feudal abbeys where 'more room was left for human nature to satisfy its appetites for pleasure and for power'.[7]

At the start the movement was a male one, and although individual Cistercians might encourage female vocations the order as a whole did not accept the idea of a Cistercian nun. But by the 1190s the general chapter was forced to take notice of the claims of certain nunneries to be Cistercian, and in 1213 these were placed under the tutelage of neighbouring monasteries. The official attitude remained discouraging but it was a triumph of female persistence that in the end twenty-seven English nunneries became Cistercian, while in France and Spain they followed Cistercian custom to the extent of holding provincial chapters on the precedent of the general chapter at Cîteaux. Recent scholarship is beginning to show us the importance of the writings of some of these women, such as Beatrice of Nazareth, for example, and undoubtedly we shall come to know more as research yields up further names and work.

The *conversi*, or lay brothers, formed a most significant element of the Cistercian order. These men represented a purely practical solution to an otherwise insoluble problem. The gifts of property that the Cistercians received were generally marginal land since more fruitful and fertile sites had already been occupied. These large stretches of moorland, of forest or waste presented problems since the Cistercians refused to have tenants and serfs and they could not afford to pay hired labourers. Thus, as the *Exordium Parvum* tells us so delightfully, 'the new recruits debated among themselves by what exercise of brains or brawn they might provide for themselves and for the guests, rich and poor, whom the Rule bids us receive as Christ'. They made the decision

to receive bearded laybrothers with the permission of their

bishop, and to treat them in life and in death as themselves, except for the monastic state. They also determined
to employ hired workmen. Without such aids they could
see no way of fully observing the precepts of the Rule,
both day and night.[8]

In order to emphasise their separation from the monks they
wore a modest beard, not to exceed more than two fingers in
length, while the monks were clean shaven or tonsured. They
wore a habit which was different in colour and cut, a basic,
simple robe, with belt, socks and footwear, and extra clothing
for certain jobs – leather for herdsmen and shepherds who
would be outside in cold weather, and mittens for the black-
smiths. These *conversi* may have been illiterate peasants with
no skill in book learning but that does not mean that they
were therefore devoid of native wit or natural culture – or of
religious sensibility, as can be seen in this charming contemporary story of the drover's helpmeet.

There was another brother in the monastery who worked
as a drover, a simple man and pure of heart. He once in
his sleep had the quite delightful vision of Our Lord Jesus
Christ beside him on the other side of the pole, holding
the goad in his own sweet hand and driving the oxen with
him. Straight after this he fell ill, took to his bed and
ended his life after six days of pain and travail. Brother
Bernard, reflecting on the vision that the monk had
related, and knowing him to be pure and simple of heart,
rejoiced exceedingly and declared confidently that the
brother walked with God. Since God had worked at his
side, he had translated him, for infinite Compassion could
not desert in his last agony the servant he had so cour-
teously toiled alongside in the field.[9]

This is taken from some of those collections of edifying
stories that were compiled in these early days, many of which
concern simple monks, named and nameless. These were men
who brought the knowledge of their hands to the looking after

of sheep or bees or vines. Many were master-craftsmen when they joined. Many had particular skills in engineering, or were specialists in waterway construction. Their commercial expertise proved invaluable in striking bargains for the community at the local fairs and markets where agricultural goods, especially wool, had to be sold.[10]

In their almost aggressive colonisation of the land, their huge expansion, their intellectual vitality, their creation of new institutions, the Cistercians were very much in tune with the century that saw their birth. It was almost as though Europe had come to life again after the sleep – or the guarding of the light – in the Dark Ages. The twelfth century was a vibrant and energetic period, pushing out its boundaries in all directions. In the schools which were to become the great universities of Europe a new era of learning was beginning, often called the Renaissance of the twelfth century. Translations of hitherto unknown works of the classical period were reaching Europe for the first time, and wandering scholars sought out all the different masters of the day, at first in one place and then another, to listen to ideas being exchanged with the new tools of logical analysis and rational argument. In the practical world new skills and technologies were being developed. With no major wars to claim attention but exciting initiatives in every direction, it was a dynamic and energising time in which to be alive. It was not surprisingly a time of self-questioning, a search for identity, and one which did not leave the religious orders untouched. The Cistercians were not the only ones to explore new forms of monasticism, to cater for the diversity of a population which doubled between 1050 and 1200, bringing into being new classes and new interests. For the first time for centuries there was room for many different kinds of life. We watch the growth of variety in the different forms and orders, the 'many rooms' within the one house. In every area of life new frontiers were being opened up, horizons broadened. The optimism was tremendous: they knew that they were standing on the shoulders of giants and could see further than them!

Influenced by the intellectual revival of their day, though standing apart from the rational approach of the schoolmen, the Cistercians studied ancient texts as fresh and living books. So they returned to the Rule of Benedict as to the wellspring, as they believed, of the monastic ideal. Even their habits of white undyed cloth made a statement about the return to purity of the original monastic vision which they felt had been lost. To regain the true ideal of the Rule and to be true to their vocation meant truth without compromise and without reserve. This passionate desire for truth was the very heart of the Cistercian reform, and one which they applied at every level of their lives, sometimes almost obsessively. Stephen Harding made his own Latin revision of the Scriptures, consulting rabbinical scholars in order to solve difficulties in the text and sending some of his monks across the Alps to Milan, to copy what he thought would be the original texts of the Gregorian antiphonal and the Ambrosian hymnal. 'He wanted to make sure that his monks were singing what had actually been revealed by God.'[11]

The underlying impulse was their sole desire to live out the essence of the Rule itself as they believed it should be lived. Benedict had said that nothing was to be preferred to the love of Christ, and now they wanted to make that gospel of love the one immediate reality of their lives, not only in letter but in spirit. Love is the keystone of the Rule, and they found a key text in verses 45–7 of the Prologue where Benedict says the monk is to foster charity, not merely to preserve it or to keep it in good working order. So, as they explained in the *Charter of Charity* they had good reason for the name 'because . . . it had for its object charity alone . . . We wish . . . that we may live united by one charity, one Rule.'

When Gilbert of Hoyland was preaching a sermon on love to a community of nuns he began by saying that love is the foundation to which we return all the time, familiar yet always new:

> You desire to hear something new,
> but I have no news
> except that love should renew you.
> This commandment is the news I give you;
> nothing is more known to you,
> yet nothing is more new.[12]

The essence of their life was Christ himself, and if Christ, as Bernard pointed out with characteristic Cistercian logic, the Incarnate Word, came to this earth to express Truth in all things by his life, passion, death and resurrection, then the monk too should live as Christ lived on earth. 'But Christ's life was poor and obscure, a life of suffering and labour and hardship, embraced, of course, not out of sheer economic necessity, but freely, for the love of God.' Whatever was superfluous was a disfigurement of the simple human self and should therefore be rejected. Above all they wanted to regain the place of manual work so that then they could be poor and live by the labour of their hands, for this was the way that the Rule said a genuine monk was supposed to live. Aelred was moved at the sight of knights and nobles working like the peasants:

> Are we not beholding nobility turning its back on the world in answer to the call to conversion, casting aside swords and spears in order to join with us as we earn our bread with the work of our hands, just as though they were the true serfs [*quasi rusticos*]?

How hard this might be can be seen in what Aelred tells us of a brother who accompanied him to Revesby, no doubt so that he could keep a fatherly eye on him when he was finding the life too demanding:

> Everything goes against the grain with me, the daily chores and my whole surroundings irk me beyond bearing. The length of the night office is a torment to me, I often collapse under the manual labour, the food sticks in my

mouth, more bitter than wormwood, and the coarse clothing bites through skin and flesh to the very bone.[13]

But beyond this, beyond any outward expression of poverty or simplicity, lay the ideal of a life whose purpose was to form the monk into the perfect likeness of Christ. In 1951, when Merton was teaching the scholastics at Gethsemani, Kentucky (the younger men still in training who were under him as their novice master), he told them how 'this perseverance, day after day, in the routine trials and difficulties of monastic life conforms us to Christ on the Cross,' and he concluded, 'hold fast to the knowledge of Christ crucified, the example of Christ, the pure love of Christ.'[14] The goal of the whole Cistercian way was, as it was for Benedict, simply Christ himself. Christ is to reign in us, Aelred told his monks, to be a pilgrim in us, we are united with him in his death and renewed in him in his resurrection.

'Our glorious master' – these early Cistercians were motivated by the desire to serve God according to the Rule of Benedict. In a sermon on his feast day, Bernard called him 'our guide, our master, our lawgiver . . . I find delight and consolation in the very thought of him'. Aelred told his community that Benedict had established a law in his Rule,

> which, if we observe it, we will enter heaven itself, the Land of the Living, and possess it forever. In his Rule he teaches us . . . to build in our heart a spiritual tabernacle for Christ. If we observe this law we will be, as he himself says, heirs of the Kingdom of Heaven.

We have many sermons such as this from abbots who would annually remind their communities on his feast day of the saint who was leader and teacher guiding his monks with charity and discretion along the simple life-giving way of the gospel. Merton drew the attention of his scholastics in particular to the four sermons of Guerric of Igny, which he told them were of unique interest. Benedict lived wisely and he lived in God. He is not only a model for us but he has transmitted to us his way of life, so that if we live our lives wisely we live in God. Guerric likened Benedict to a tree planted by the living waters of divine wisdom. We too are happy in proportion as we sink our roots into the wisdom of God. The image of roots brings out the significance of stability, which Benedict puts first in the monastic profession, since it is foundational for everything else. There is a close connection between fruitfulness and stability, and no monk can grow in love if he does not sink his roots in his community. The tree planted by the waters of wisdom will bring forth fruit if we give it time, if we keep silence, if we have the humility to see that we cannot do everything ourselves.

In one of his sermons on Benedict, Aelred made a parallel with Moses: 'Blessed Benedict, following the example of Blessed Moses, went and "fled away and dwelt in solitude" [Psalm 54:8]' where God appeared to him in the bush and in the fire. In the bush are thorns, Aelred told the monks, in the fire, heat and splendour, which are three signs:

> In the thorns we see temptation,
> in the heat, love,
> and in the splendour, contemplation . . .
> Temptation teaches compassion,
> love teaches solicitude,
> contemplation teaches prudence.
> So I can safely entrust myself to you,
> most blessed father Benedict,
> who in your temptation learned
> 'to have compassion on my weaknesses' [Hebrews 4:15]
> who, as you burn with the fire of charity,
> know just what are my needs.[15]

Chrysogonus Waddell, a monk of Gethsemani, thinks of what the experience of a novice might have been in the twelfth century as he imagines a young man whom he calls Ernaut of Veretz, who after going to Paris and hearing first Abelard and then Bernard, joins the community at Clairvaux. He describes life in the novitiate – no doubt writing out of his own experience as a novice 800 years later – the daily round of mass and office, hard work in the fields, and instruction, consisting of the Rule with commentary.

> The enthusiastic love these White Monks had for the Holy Rule was something that Ernaut only gradually came to understand; for it was only by living the Rule day after day, and by feeling his life transformed from within by it that, by degrees, Ernaut came to love the Rule. The Rule did more than to establish a honorarium and provide the outward structures and principal observance of the life. It provided, of course, a spiritual doctrine that was the encapsulation of the whole New Testament; but more importantly, it provided a practical program whereby the Gospel realities could be interiorised and made dynamically effective in the life of the monk.

The balanced life of prayer, study and work became a unity as Ernaut found that each part interpenetrated the other:

> Whether chanting the psalms, receiving the eucharist, doing his daily spiritual reading, or praying in the silence of his heart while swinging a mattock in the woodshed Ernaut was celebrating the Mystery of Christ.

This Christ, on whom the Rule is centred, gradually becomes the centre of his own life, so that he 'comes to live Christ, and to love him intimately'.[16]

Isaac of Stella expresses it very simply and beautifully:

> He himself is my meditation;
> he is my delight;
> him for his own sake I seek above me;
> from him himself I feed within me.
> He is the field in which I labour;
> he is the fruit for which I labour.
> He is my cause;
> he is my effect.
> He is my beginning;

he is my end without end.
He is for eternity.[17]

The elegance, wisdom and prayer-filled quality of early Cistercian writing can be seen in passages such as this. It is a *bon mot* to say that although they gave up many things they did not give up the art of writing well. The austerity of their architecture does not apply to their literary style. It seemed to be second nature to men like Bernard, or Aelred of Rievaulx, William of St Thierry, Gilbert of Hoyland, Guerric of Igny, whose writings will appear time and again in this book, to produce, apparently spontaneously, words of consummate beauty. Here is an example in Gilbert of Hoyland where he is meditating on the passion, one of the foundation stones of the monk's life, with tenderness and profound depths of sensibility.

> The softest of pillows for me, good Jesus,
> is that crown of thorns from your head.
> A welcome little bed is that wood of your Cross.
> On this I am bred and born,
> created and re-created
> and upon the altars of your passion
> I gladly rebuild for myself
> the nest of memory.[18]

'The rich and elegant vitality of Cistercian prose – most of which is sheer poetry' is how Thomas Merton characterised twelfth-century Cistercian writing. Many of these men would have been steeped in secular literary movements before they entered the cloister, unlike the Benedictine communities who frequently took children as oblates and educated them within the monastery. But if contact with the currents of classical humanism then sweeping Europe stimulated intellectual excitement the monks had to reconcile this with the perspective of the cloister, and with the contemplative approach of monastic vocation. They knew Ovid but they also knew another way of another love; they knew the subtleties of Plato and Aristotle, but they also knew how the school of the Holy Spirit teaches not by words but by grace. The conflict between secular and Christian humanism caught them up into the sort of dialectic that was a source of vitality, and the rather intense intellectual life that we find forming at Clairvaux or at Rievaulx, for example, was the result of the juncture of these particular forces.

Of course they would never deny that the highest knowledge of God is the knowledge that is directly communicated to the soul in mystical experience, and that this is a knowledge that cannot be arrived at by human efforts. Merton tells how Aelred arrived at the personal intimate contact with truth itself not merely as an intellectual certainty but in the wholeness of an experience that called into play all the deepest powers of his being. 'One of the tests of a true contemplative is his simplicity. A contemplation that expresses itself in an elaborate and subtle and peculiar system of thought, involved and complex and laborious to unravel, is always suspect.' But while, as Walter Daniel, Aelred's biographer, tells us, he did not obscure the truth under a flood of useless words or subtle concepts, he did not make an affectation of rusticity. He spoke eloquently and clearly. His style was fluid and impassioned; every line he wrote was alive and supple. Merton knew, as the master of scholastics in charge of the intellectual formation of the young men at Gethsemani, that serious theological study is of immense importance in the formation of the contemplative life. In a monastery in which study is neglected contemplation is also generally at rather a low ebb. A solid contemplative life requires a real theological foundation.[19] It is a nice thought, which Merton gives us in a footnote, that the monks of Cluny got Livy and Cicero for their Lenten books.

Why should men and women today want to follow the Cistercian path? There are at present 2,557 Cistercian monks in ninety-six monasteries and 1,883 Cistercian nuns in sixty-six houses throughout the world. In North America alone there are now over forty communities. It is impressive to read through a yearbook which lists the number of houses in Ethiopia or India or Japan. When I stayed in Japan in a Cistercian community it was an amazing sight to watch over eighty women as they came into vespers, all wearing cowls, all more or less the same height, in a seemingly endless procession. The essentials of the life remain the same; the externals are moving with the times. Manual labour today may be the making of the bread and fruit cake which are both very popular monastic products, but it may also be using word processors to do such work as cataloguing some of the big libraries in America.

Many lay people feel the attraction of this distinctive Cistercian charism, above all because of its essential simplicity and the central place that it gives to contemplative prayer. Communities with guesthouses are being sought out by those who are hungry for places of silence and prayer which they cannot find within the structures of the institutional church. Basil Pennington speaks of the attraction of time spent with a monastic community, which visitors immediately sense:

> A Cistercian monastery is a place of silence, a place where one can find the quiet to hear. A Cistercian monastery is a place of freedom, where all is ordered to free us so that we can listen and respond to the deepest aspiration of our being. Cistercian simplicity does not apply only to our striking architecture with its chaste unadorned beauty and our plainchant. Modest diet and a practical spartan wardrobe, along with freedom from radio and television and the distraction of travel and visits, all contribute to allowing the monk to cultivate through study, meditation, prayer, and work guided by obedience a mind and heart totally orientated toward God – in simplicity.[20]

It is a commonplace to speak of the monastic life as marginal. But does this mean, as so many people tend to assume, that this is a life of escape, of isolation? What Henri Nouwen experienced at the end of his seven months' stay, living alongside the community at Genesee, was that he had not only come closer to God, he had come closer to the world as well. When the abbot asked him to give his impressions to the brothers in chapter this was his first point:

> My stay at the monastery has not only brought me closer
> to Christ, it has brought me closer to the world as well.
> In fact, distance from the world has made me feel more
> compassionate toward it. In my work at home I am so
> busy with immediate needs asking for an immediate
> response that my world narrows down to my daily worries,
> and I lost perspective on the larger problems. Here . . . I
> become more intimately aware of the pain and suffering
> of the whole world . . .

And then, speaking of what the support of the community had
meant, he said 'God is the hub of the wheel of life. The closer
we come to God the closer we come to each other.'[21]

The mysterious way in which this apparently hidden life
carries power can be seen as we read the story of the life of Sr
Maria Gabriella, one of the many thousands of Cistercian men
and women who live quietly obedient and faithful lives of
prayer and who in general remain unknown and unnamed.
She was born of peasant stock in Sardinia in 1914, and in
1935, at the age of twenty-one, entered the small, crowded and
poor convent of Grottaferrata. Outwardly nothing could be
more ordinary. In her very simple letters to her family we can
see how what might seem to an outsider the banality of her
life gave her daily a thousand ways to learn the dying to self-
will and the growth of love for others and for God. Here was
a woman who passed unnoticed in the common life and yet as
Jean Leclercq said, 'like so many unknown nuns who will
never be spoken of she assimilated the spiritual riches of a
tradition which she lived'. As the contemplative life grew
within her and the rhythm of the monastic life clarified her
sight and sharpened her will, she began above all to learn
something of unity, at first in her own self, for she had been a
wilful, headstrong child and adolescent. But as she now slowly
came to identify with Christ's love, she found a love that re-
conciles and heals, bringing unity. This then broadened out
and, knowing nothing of any details of schism or divides within
the Church, on 31 October 1937, the feast of Christ the King,

she made her offering for unity, 'my little offering, because I am united with You, and for my part, I have given all that it is in my power to give'. Until then she had never been ill. Yet within a matter of weeks she developed what proved to be galloping consumption which was declared to be terminal. Gabriella accepted this as an answer to her prayer. 'My will is of no consequence,' she would say; 'whatever God wills is good for me. Whether I live or die is unimportant.' Fifteen months later in April 1939 this utterly simple and silent woman died – but her work for unity, thanks to the connection with the Abbé Paul Couturier, has lived on. The prayer written about her, which is used in the cause of unity, opens with words which summarise her life and vocation: 'Lord, You choose things small and insignificant, things fragile and poor, in order that they be signs of your saving power . . .'[22]

In this she tells us much about other Cistercian men and women who over the centuries have given themselves up to a life of prayer. For in the end it is, as it has always been, the secret, hidden life of prayer that is the most significant thing about the Cistercian way. That is why our Lady held such a strong place in their hearts – the humble, hidden young woman whose response of obedience to the calling of God gave them the role model for their own hidden obedient lives. They carried, as she did, the Word in their hearts and pondered Christ in lives of contemplation, as she did. Their white habit recalled purity, her symbol. All Cistercian churches are dedicated to her. Every day ends with the singing of the Salve Regina, the hymn to her. At Dore Abbey one of the bosses from the roof nave shows an abbot holding his abbatial staff, kneeling before the Mother who with her left hand supports the child standing on her knees dressed in a long loose tunic, still with traces of red paint. It is a delicate and touching scene: Mary's right hand holds her child's right hand and in his left hand he has a small orb (or could it be a bird, as it is in the window of a nearby Herefordshire church?). A *Tract on the Blessed Mary* written at Dore in the mid-thirteenth century, probably just a few years earlier than this carving, expresses the same quality of gentle humanity. It is by Cadwgan who came to Dore in 1236 to end his life there as a simple monk after being abbot of Whitland and Bishop of Bangor, so that he might have more time for spiritual writing:

> She went up into the hill country of Juda with haste,
>   entered into the house of Zacharias,
>   and saluted Elizabeth.
> She went up out of Nazareth,
>   together with Joseph,
>   unto Bethlehem.
> She went up into the Temple of the Lord,
>   together with Joseph,
>   that she might place her Child,
>   in the presence of the Lord.
> She went up out of Egypt,
>   together with Joseph,
>   into the land of Israel.
> She went up to Jerusalem that she might pray
>   together with Joseph,
>   after the custom of the feast.
> She went up again to Jerusalem,
>   together with Joseph,
>   that she might seek the Child Jesus.
> She went up at length into heaven,
>   to take her place by her blessed Son.
>   'Upon thy right hand did stand the queen.'
>   (Psalm 45)

> The first ascension, was to visit and to minister,
> The second, to beget and to obey,
> The third, to present her Son, and to offer a pair of
>   turtle doves and two young pigeons.
> The fourth, to keep vigil, and to make her dwelling,
> The fifth, to pray.
> The sixth, to seek her Child, and to find Him.
> The seventh, to have joy and to reign.[23]

A fresco in Forde Abbey tells us something of the place that Mary held in their hearts, for, as in this piece from Dore, we are shown the very human face of Mary. She stands at the foot of the cross, a vibrant young woman with long, flowing golden hair, spreading over her shoulders and down her back. She is wearing a red cloak with clasps and very full sleeves. She is serene, almost self-contained. She is half turned, so that she seems to be sharing the agony of watching her dying son with those also standing close by – the monks who had placed this not in their chapel but in their dormitory undercroft, probably around 1320.[24]

Here is the woman who is 'our lady, our advocate, our helper', as Aelred said to his monks in a sermon preached on the feast of the Assumption; 'think of how much confidence we can have in her':

> Let us lift up our eyes to heaven,
> let us not forget her mercy.
> Let us confidently beseech her and place our trust in
>   her . . .
> Let her be our common joy,
> our common glory,
> our common hope,
> our common consolation,
> our common reconciliation,
> and our common refuge.
> If we are sad, let us fly to her so that she may gladden
>   us.
> If we are disheartened, let us fly to her so that she may
>   make us cheerful.
> If we are in despair, let us fly to her so that she may
>   raise us up.
> If we are troubled, let us fly to her so that she may
>   console us.
> If we are suffering persecutions, let us fly to her so that
>   she may protect us.

> If we are at odds with her son, let us fly to her so that
>   she may reconcile us.
> Let her be our guardian in this life and our protection at
>   death.
> May she protect us from sin even now,
>   and later may she present us to her beloved son.[25]

Whenever Aelred speaks about Mary, his intent is to convey to his listeners that her life can and should be imitated, since it perfectly illustrates the ideal monastic life. Many of the sermons that we have were preached on the feast of the Assumption, when each year the entire monastic community, choir-monks and lay brothers, would assemble together for their annual patronal festival on 15 August. As they listened to the Gospel for the day, the story of Mary and Martha, the two sisters dwelling together in the house at Bethany, they would think of how the Blessed Virgin brought those two women together in herself, the active and the contemplative, and so gave them a role model for their own vocation. They saw her active perfection; her contemplation lay in her silence, in keeping the words of God in her heart. Her *fiat* was her greatest work, and therefore the culmination of all that we can call her 'active life'. But the incarnation itself took place in the secrecy of her contemplative solitude, when she received into her bosom the Word of God. Contemplation and action were in her all one, perfectly united in the mystery of her divine motherhood.

But then she is also the Queen of Heaven, and as Bernard reminded his listeners in one of his sermons for this same feast, 'We are obliged to believe that she has been exalted above all the angelic choirs, above even the cherubim and seraphim, and the joy of the angels.' So there is this further important aspect: the feast of the Assumption is an eschatological experience, which celebrates the continuity between earth and heaven, between the earthly love of Mary who loved Christ after the flesh, and the love which is consummated in heaven, when she is able to love him after the spirit. Here again

Mary is the perfect monastic model, not only in the historical particularity of her life but in its eschatological fulfilment celebrated in this annual festival.

But in the end it was the inner dynamism of her life that was important. In her they found the virtues that they themselves espoused, her faith, her chastity, humility and charity and, above all, her obedience. She was a model in her initial act of obedience, a virtue foundational in the monastic life. Her life was a story of obedient love from beginning to end. Here was this woman who lived as they also try to live, at the heart of the mystery of salvation.[26]

3. THE WORD

Prayer lies at the heart of the Cistercian life; the essential activity, which in the end becomes the only activity, is a life of prayer. What nourishes this, keeps it alive and renews it daily and yearly, is the Word of God. The Word must be heard in the silence of the heart, the place in which it can be welcomed and given space so that it may become creative. From the earliest time the advice given by any monastic father to a disciple who wanted to learn the monastic way was always 'return to your own heart'. This is the interior space for which there are so many differing concepts: the inner cloister, the *poustinia*, the cave of the heart. It is simply 'the place of God in us' which each of us will understand in a unique and mysterious way.

Every day, therefore, begins by entering into that secret and hidden space in order to hear the Word. The Cistercian daily schedule meant rising early, while it was still dark, for the first office of the day, Vigils, sometimes called Matins. Times would vary between winter and summer, but an approximate pattern might be something like this: Vigils was sung at some time between midnight and 4 a.m., Lauds followed at dawn, and the morning was split by the three shorter offices of Prime, Terce and Sext. Mass was celebrated after Terce in winter, before in summer. The afternoon hours were None, at 2 p.m., and Vespers, with Compline closing the day around 6.30 p.m. Therefore, when the community would be roused by the sound of a bell in the small hours of the following morning and would immediately descend by way of the night stairs into the choir, they would have had a full eight hours of rest. The

Rule says that 'by sleeping until a little past the middle of the night the brothers can arise with their food fully digested' (ch. 8). Starting the day in the darkness of the night and going from darkness into light was a daily reminder of the movement from dark to light. It was a symbolic enactment of the paschal mystery itself, taking us from sleep and death to new life, from the cross to resurrection.

As the monk keeps guard, alert and attentive like the careful virgins of the Gospel, he is standing on the frontier between what is passing and what lies ahead, looking towards the coming of Christ. But this vigilance is a keeping guard, not only for themselves but for a sleeping world. Morning after morning they proclaim by this commitment how urgent it is to draw the world from its sleep so that it too can go out and meet Christ, coming like the bridegroom – for we do not do justice to Vigils unless we emphasise its joyous character, the festal shout of the Last Day, the dawn that will never end: 'Come Lord Jesus!'

In the silence of the night Vigils opens with the words 'Lord, open my lips and my mouth shall proclaim your praise', said three times, after which follow a long series of psalms, each followed by a reading, but always the first psalm will be Psalm 3:

> I lie down to rest, and I sleep,
> I wake, for the Lord upholds me.

And then follows Psalm 94 (95) with its invitation to come joyfully and reverently, which in verse seven has those wonderful words which sum up the start of day for any of us: 'O that today you would listen to my voice', the daily reminder that every day God speaks to us, if we are ready to listen, and to listen, in the words of Benedict, 'with the ear of the heart'. The experience of the people of Israel in the desert showed how easy it is to harden the heart, to grumble at God, to forget to listen.

This listening comes above all in the regular saying of the psalms, and in the reading of Scripture. The pattern of the office of Vigils is repeated throughout the day as the community comes together at regular intervals, interrupting whatever they may be doing for the one thing which claims priority, and around which their life revolves, the opus Dei, the work of God. The office of Lauds brings the community together again at the hour of the sun's rising and is generally followed by the eucharist; as the working day now begins, the offices become rather shorter until with evening comes the office of Vespers, and finally Compline, to make the day complete. With the singing of the Salve Regina, the community commends itself to the safe keeping of our Lady and then retires to bed.

After he had spent several months living with the Cistercian community of the Genesee in the USA, Henri Nouwen reflected in his diary how much the psalms had come to mean to him through this daily usage in the liturgical round of the offices. Compline became for him one of the most intimate and prayerful moments of the monastic day, particularly since the words were always the same and no books or lights were needed. He began to realise how the psalms 'slowly become flesh in me':

> Slowly these words enter into the center of my heart. They are more than ideas, images, comparisons. They become a real presence ... Many times I have thought: If I am ever sent to prison, if I am ever subjected to hunger, pain, torture, or humiliation, I hope and pray that they let me keep the psalms. The psalms will keep my spirit alive ... Maybe I should start learning the psalms by heart so that nobody can take them away from me.[1]

In this he was discovering for himself something central to the Cistercian tradition. In a medieval community the novices were expected to memorise the Psalter. Throughout the history of monasticism the psalms have formed the mainstay of prayer. What was said of Wulfstan – *semper in ore psalmus: semper in corde Christus*: 'His mouth was always filled with psalms, his heart was filled with Christ' – is an aphorism true of any Cistercian. Michael Casey, the prior of the Australian community in Tarrawarra, speaks of this in terms of the building up of a friendship, which is something that is bound to take time:

> You will never grasp the meaning of the Psalms of David until, through experience, you make his sentiments your own ... There is the same gulf between attentive study and mere perusal as there is between friendship and acquaintance with a transient, or between close affection and a passing word of greeting.[2]

He then goes on to speak of 'the rugged and concrete emotiveness of the psalms' compared with the slick informational functionality of language today. They must be understood as poetry – as prayers in poetry, with their own peculiar nuances and rhythm and above all their range of images. The monk does not cut them up into parts, segments, but embraces them whole. The Rule asks for the whole Psalter to be prayed; Benedict does not select in the way that we do today. One of the things that the psalms can do for us is to reveal to us hidden aspects of our own reality. In the image used by Athanasius, they are like a mirror in which we suddenly catch a glimpse of something of our own inner processes. 'There can be no prayer of any depth until we have descended into our own depths.' Matthew Kelty, a monk of Gethsemani and a friend of Merton, said in a sermon in the 1960s that in entering the world of the psalms we touch human nature on all its levels. He even called them a dangerous form of prayer! For while they are often songs of thanksgiving and rejoicing, joyous and benign, they can also bring us face to face with the conflict within us, with the demons within our own hearts:

> For when you take the psalms seriously and receive their spirit as your own, when you live what they live and experience what they experience, you come very soon into contact with some basic realities about human nature. The psalms are not all nature hymns and marching

tunes ... There is also darkness, wrath and anger, hatred and vengeance, and a host of other unhappy qualities in the heart of a person ... The psalms can teach us much of the conflict with evil within us.[3]

The universality of the psalms is a tremendous source of strength. It is not only that I remember that they were the journey songs of the people of Israel in the past, but I can remind myself of all the monastic communities, parish priests, people living alone, who will be making them their daily prayer. Henry Vaughan's lines about daybreak, 'the whole creation shakes off night', come alive as I think of the time lag as the sun moves from east to west with this continuous wave of prayer. Sometimes the psalms enable us to express anguish or anger, sometimes they remind us of steadfastness and confidence, or gratitude and rejoicing, sometimes we may seem dead and they arouse no spark of response. Basil Pennington, another contemporary Cistercian, writes of the differing levels at which we can approach them:

> We can always make the words of the psalmist our own and enter into them as best we can. We can also hear them as the words of Christ himself, who so often prayed these psalms, and let him now pray them within us and speak to us through them. We can also hear them as the words of the psalmist speaking to us about Christ our God and join with him in his prayer and praise.[4]

This is the crux of it all: to pray the Psalter with Christ. Time and again this is the message. Matthew Kelty puts it succinctly: 'To my mind, unless we pray the psalter with Jesus we had better not pray it at all.' In the psalms, Thomas Merton said, 'We sing of our experience of God ... contemplation of God in the Mystery of Christ ... the psalms form our minds and direct our thoughts and affections to God, but they establish us in God, they unite us to Him in Christ.' When he was teaching the novices at Gethsemani in 1955 he put it in terms of being attuned to the psalms:

If we are attuned to the meaning of the psalms we feel their healing power as we recite them in choir. We must be attuned to the experience of the inspired writer and relive it in ourselves. The deep reason for this is that Christ is the physician who heals all our infirmities. In proportion as we 'touch him in the scriptures' we are healed by him. So we go to them to enter into contact with him. His word heals. 'Say the word and my servant shall be healed.'[5]

In the Middle Ages the psalms, like the Bible, were glossed, with explanatory notes and patristic explications written in smaller script between the lines and in the generous margins. Imagining what it would have been like in the twelfth century, another American Cistercian today says that 'the psalm coming with its exegetical explanation would plunge the monk into the context of the whole panoramic Mystery of Christ', until they saw 'the whole of Scripture illuminated by the light of the Paschal Candle'.[6] But then this was equally true of the whole Bible, the monk's book par excellence. He used it easily and naturally, as one of God's greater gifts; he rejoiced at the mysteries it enshrined, above all the mystery of Christ. It was for him something living, life-giving. It is interesting to reflect how this comes about – not through long solitary reading but through exposure to the liturgy and to the Fathers. That their use of the Bible should be profoundly influenced by the cycle of the liturgical readings is not after all so very surprising when one reflects that several hours were spent daily at the work of God, the opus Dei, and this could hardly fail to be formative of their spirituality. By following the liturgical calendar they followed the major events of Christ's life, not just in some remote or pious fashion, but entering into the saving meaning of that life. From the nativity to the passion, year by year they would be reminded that our redemption takes place through the birth and death of the God-man Christ.

He was incomprehensible and inaccessible,
invisible and completely unthinkable.

Now he wishes to be comprehended,
wishes to be seen,
wishes to be thought about.
How, do you ask?
As lying in the manger,
resting in the Virgin's lap,
preaching on the mountain,
praying through the night,
or hanging on the cross,
growing pale in death,
free among the dead and ruling in hell,
and also as rising on the third day,
showing the apostles the place of the nails,
the signs of victory,
and finally as ascending over heaven's secrets in their
    sight.[7]

They searched the Scriptures for light on the things that have always preoccupied the Church: the great doctrines of the incarnation and redemption which, as Thomas Merton says, lie at the very heart of revelation and which are the key to all the vital problems of human and moral existence. They have no wish to pursue subtle, fascinating textual problems. André Louf has written of the possibility that the distinction between Cistercian theology and that of the academic schools is explainable in terms of a difference between right-brain and left-brain thinking, the former more artistic, intuitive, integrative thought, the latter analytical and logical.

In a letter to a student called Adam, Gilbert of Hoyland tried to draw the young man away from the scholarship of the schools, which he called futile, chasing shadows, becoming 'warped by Aristotelian arguments'. He wished that he would instead turn to 'the veiled and mystic meanings' by which we are changed, and transmuted into a new person, 'reaching up right into the mind of Christ, in whom are hidden all the treasures of God's wisdom'.[8] Scripture had for them an almost sacramental character. Hidden in the outward appearance of the 'letter' was the deep grace implanted there by God himself. Walter Daniel tells us that as Aelred of Rievaulx lay dying he gathered round him twenty or thirty of the monks and from his bedside discussed 'the spiritual delights of the Scriptures'.[9]

The Cistercian approach was that of the wisdom tradition of the Bible, with its theme of God's wisdom over against human foolishness. Wisdom was the foundation of all that was made, the foundation of the city of God which is the Church. Wisdom was with God, arranging all things. 'When he laid out the foundations of the earth, I was by his side, a master craftsman, delighting him day after day, ever at play in his presence, at play everywhere in his world, delighting to be with the sons of men' (Proverbs 8:30). This is wonderfully imaginative and poetic, playful in the connections it makes, in the role given to imagery and symbol. Bernard makes use of all the wisdom symbols: bread, water, perfume, fruits, tree of life, fountain, jewels, and while his use of wisdom is quite traditional, at the same time he manages to bring to it his own interpretation, the fruits of his own knowledge and love, and not least his own experience, particularly as abbot, which he depicts as that of a nurturing mother. It is almost as though he himself performs the role of wisdom, by teaching us, leading us on, helping us to love God's creation and God himself. 'She leads humanity to God's bliss.'[10]

The Cistercian writers make Scripture so much their own that half of what they say is scriptural quotation. Like all the other monastic writers of the early days they had absorbed Scripture to the point where they actually did their thinking in the very terms of the prophets and evangelists. We can see it particularly clearly in the case of Bernard himself, where not only his whole inner being but also his teaching, his language and his images are all saturated with the scriptures. Michael Casey has estimated that in Bernard's sermons on the Song of Songs there is one scriptural citation for every two lines of text, and Bernard himself tells us that when he quoted Scripture he depended on his memory, not a verbal memory but rather a general sense of the passage. 'I quoted, as I

thought, the text and then found that it was not in the Gospel
at all, I had no intention of falsifying the text but I was
depending on my memory of the general sense of the passage
and made a slip in the words.'

The Bible was clearly also the main source of inspiration for
all the twelfth-century Cistercian writers, and it is often difficult if not impossible to decide where the Bible ends and their
own writing begins. It is as though they wrote with pens dipped
in the ink of Scripture, and they produced meditative passages
totally woven from scriptural phrases, although the meaning
remains entirely their own. These are the opening words of
the sermon of Aelred of Rievaulx preached on the feast of the
Purification of the Blessed Virgin Mary, 2 February:

> Brothers, I see that you have gathered so that you may
> be
> fed with the food that endures [cf John 6:27],
> the saving food of God's word.
> This is the bread that came down from heaven
> and gives life to the world [John 6:33].
> You ask for this bread just like the children of the Lord
> Jesus.
> By coming here you wish to be fed,
> especially with the bread that fills the mind more than
> the stomach,
> lest you fall behind on the road [cf. Matthew 15:32].
> May the Lord grant that he be the one who breaks it for
> you,
> so that it may not be said about you:
> The little children have asked for bread,
> and there was none to break it for them [Lamentations
> 4:4].[11]

Later on in that same sermon he goes on to speak of 'the
bread of your pilgrimage in the mystery of Christ's Incarnation'
as the possession of a joy ' . . . that eye has not seen or ear heard
or the human heart conceived', quoting from 1 Corinthians 2:9.
That small phrase 'the possession of a joy' manages to catch

something of the sense of refreshment, even excitement, that I have found in my reading of the Cistercian fathers, which is so unlike most of the theology I read today. Hilary Costello, monk of Mount St Bernard, has said that symbolic theology is arguably the most powerful type of theology, since it strikes at the guts rather than the head, and appeals to the whole person, to feeling and to moods as well as to the intellect. The problem is that while today we have lost touch with all those symbols taken for granted in the past, many now trivialised or weakened (especially by their use in advertising), many people are still longing for such a theology. It is as though there is hunger to reclaim the poetic and the artistic side of ourselves. I have found myself led much more deeply into prayer, a prayer that has the character of poetry and song, by the way in which the Cistercians used language. Gilbert of Hoyland described how the kernel differs from the shell:

> What sweetness lies in the kernel,
> if so much is seen in the shell!
> Mysteries lie hidden to be dug out with effort,
> but the charm of the words is on the surface,
> offered gratuitously,
> slipping without effort into pure souls.
> Now we do not give so much attention to the mysteries
> as to disregard the melody,
> for these are songs
> and prefer to be sung rather than debated,
> and I doubt whether they can be analysed more clearly
> than when they are sung.[12]

For they were not so much concerned with the literal sense of a text as anxious to leave the husk in order to get at the inner meat, the typological meaning. 'Let us try to draw out the spiritual fruit which lies underneath the rind of the letter,' as Bernard said of the Song of Songs. 'I will search for the treasure of the spirit and life hidden in the profound depths of these inspired utterances.' The mysteries hidden beneath the words have to be dug out, in silence, taking time, for only then can we recover those hidden layers of meaning. John of Forde called the Bible a wood which had its thickets, where dense mysteries could be found, and he said, in a familiar medieval comparison, that it was like a mirror in which the image alters as one holds it near or away from oneself. There are various levels of meaning and one ought to move quickly to the inner levels. The analogy that he used was of the wine-cellar:

> The words of wisdom are rich in senses, like a rich man's wine-cellar . . . There is softer wine and stronger wine for those more eminent in understanding and more capable of drinking. There is wine which he mixes for his friends, that which he offers to his dearest friends, that which he presses for the family, and that which he measures out for those of weaker capacity.[13]

Bernard has a much more complex map for this interior journey. He gives us a succession of locations, each of which represents a level of reading that must be personally appropriated. 'Let the garden be the plain and simple historical sense, the cellar the moral sense, the bridal chamber the mystery of visionary contemplation.' He works this out in detail, and it all becomes extremely complicated as we move through the smell of spices, the feel of ointment and the taste of wine while we are spending time in the cellar.

Guerric of Igny is much gentler and simpler. In a sermon 'for arousing devotion at psalmody' he told his brothers that they were

> strolling about in as many gardens as you read books, plucking as many apples as you garner meanings. And blessed are all those for whom the apples, new and old, have been stored up; for whom, that is, the words of the prophets, evangelists and apostles have been preserved, so that the assurance of the Bridegroom to the Bride – 'all the apples, new and old, I have kept for you, my beloved' – seems addressed to each one of you.

Later in the sermon he saw Jesus as the gardener in words which I have transposed into the form of a prayer:

> O Lord Jesus,
> true gardener,
> work in us what you want of us,
> for without you we can do nothing.
> For you are indeed the true gardener,
> at once the maker and tiller and keeper of your garden,
> you who plant with the word,
> water with the spirit
> and give your increase with your power.[14]

It was through Word that the twelfth-century monk came to know and love Christ. The Christ on whom the Rule is centred is the centre of Cistercian life. The liturgy does not exist for itself any more than does the Rule, or the monastic lifestyle and its institutions. That would mean worshipping an idol rather than all the time looking beyond, to the figure of Christ himself. The whole cycle of liturgical readings is about that. The whole way of life is a following of Christ, an imitation of him. Everything touched on their relationship with Christ; everything was ordered towards the totality of Christ, on earth and in heaven, as Aelred said in a sermon preached on the feast of the Assumption:

> Indeed brothers, it is a great good
> and a great joy
> to know our Lord Jesus Christ according to his humanity
> and to love him according to his humanity:
> to think about him,
> to see, as it were, in one's heart his nativity,
> his Passion,
> his wounds,
> his death,
> and his Resurrection.
> But the one who feels a far greater joy
> is the one who can say with the Apostle:

And if we knew Christ according to the flesh, we no
longer know him this way now [2 Corinthians 5:16].
. It is a great joy to consider how our Lord lay in a manger,
but it is a far greater joy to contemplate how he reigns
   in heaven,
It is a great joy to consider how he nursed at his mother's
   breasts,
but it is a far greater joy to contemplate how he feeds all
   creation.
It is a great joy to consider him in the arms of one
   maiden,
but it is a far greater joy to contemplate how he holds
within himself everything in heaven and on earth.[15]

The same theme is given very beautiful expression by Isaac
of Stella in this passage:

He himself is my meditation;
he is my delight;
him for his own sake I seek above me;
from him himself I feed within me.
He is the field in which I labour;
he is the fruit for which I labour.
He is my cause;
he is my effect.
He is my beginning;
he is my end without end.
He is for eternity.[16]

Everything helped them to discover the face of Christ so
that by gazing on him they might come to know him and
knowing him be changed, transformed into that same likeness.
The context for this is silence, as Gilbert of Hoyland explained
when he wrote to the young student Adam:

Does our silence strike you as meaningless and dead – the
silence in which this inner activity is taking place, in
which one learns and practises the art of progressing
towards God in an undeviating line by changing and trans-

muting oneself into a new man, the new Adam, and of reaching up right to the mind of Christ, in whom are hidden all the treasures of God's wisdom?[17]

The one thing that most people immediately associate with the Cistercian life is silence, and it comes as something of a shock to learn that there is no vow of silence as such. Yet silence remains a necessity, not only the great silence which runs from Compline through to the following morning but the lesser silence by which unnecessary talking is eliminated and there is a pervading atmosphere of quiet. William of St Thierry records how struck he was when he first came to Clairvaux by this astonishing picture of a community that lived in silence:

> From the moment when having come down the mountain-side I arrived at the Abbey of Clairvaux, I could sense the presence of God ... I realised that the silence here is as complete by day as it is by night, and apart from the noise of the work or the sweet sound of the praises of God, there is nothing to be heard. The effect of such silence in the midst of such activity on those who come here, is so profound that not only do they forbear from speaking idle and vain words, but they even maintain a reverent silence themselves. Even though the numbers of monks was great, each one was alone and solitary.[18]

Silence is necessary not only for listening to God but also for listening to oneself in a way that can be frightening: 'In the silence we touch our emptiness, our loneliness, our longing.' Basil Pennington is writing out of his own experience of the Cistercian life, and as a result he knows that 'In the end the monk learns that God speaks by silence and can be heard in silence. And that nothing really needs to be said. Silence is enough.'[19]

In one of his poems, 'The Trappist Cemetery – Gethsemani', Thomas Merton wrote these simple lines:

> Teach us, Cistercian Fathers, how to wear
> Silence, our humble armour.

He thought much about silence and solitude, 'the silence that is printed in the centre of our being. It will not fail us.' Throughout his monastic life, he explored what it meant and what it could give. Here, as so often, he seems to be speaking on behalf of many people today who increasingly recognise a hunger for a point of silence not only in a world of externally battering noise, but no less an inner world of clamour, which Isaac of Stella once called 'the gale in your mind'. Silence, attentiveness, ask us to take time, to handle time gently and without violence. In reading, that means to linger over words until they yield up their inner sense and then to carry them in one's heart until they become fruitful. 'Hold and touch lingeringly and lovingly', in the words of Gilbert of Hoyland:

> Hold fast to what you hold,
> hold and touch
> lingeringly and lovingly
> the word of life.
> Unroll the scroll of life,
> the scroll which Jesus unrolls,
> or rather, which is Jesus.
> Wrap yourself in him,
> wrap yourself in that fine linen in which he was wrapped
> for he was clothed as light as in a garment.
> Put on your Beloved, our Lord Jesus Christ.[20]

This idea of poring lovingly over the sacred texts of the Scriptures until it is as though we are wrapping ourselves in the Word might be taken as a description of *lectio divina* – that Latin phrase which is kept for it expresses something specific which gets lost in translation. This is slow, attentive, prayer-filled reading, which above all takes time. Aelred makes a nice parallel with friendship, about which he knew so much, saying that we must read diligently, and 'diligent reading is as far from superficial perusal as friendship is distinct from acquaintance with a stranger, or as affection given to a companion differs from a casual greeting'.[21]

Divine reading may at first sound simple but it is in fact

both deep and rich. It is not even spiritual reading, in the sense in which that phrase is used today. It is called divine because God gives us his Word directly. It is not a matter of reading things about God; God takes the initiative and intervenes; he speaks and addresses each person individually uniquely.

The word *lectio* was originally used to designate reading aloud since the monks would hear the text read aloud or would read it aloud to themselves in a low voice in the cloister. Reading in this way was a physical activity which involved listening, and thus engaged the whole person more completely. As they mumbled the words in their times of personal reading they were making them their own and interiorising them. Basil Pennington tells us how he smiled the first time he read in a letter of Peter the Venerable that he had not been able to do his *lectio* for some days because he had laryngitis!

It is usual to describe *lectio divina* in terms of four stages: *lectio* is followed by *meditatio*, *oratio* and finally leads into *contemplatio*. This is misleading if it in any way implies a technique or method, or carries the idea of reaching some goal or objective. Instead, the power at work in *lectio* belongs exclusively to the Word of God. We start by listening to the sound of God's voice, for otherwise we may miss the daily gift that he has for each of us: 'Today if you hear his voice, do not harden your heart'. So the beginning is to read slowly from some portion of Scripture (in my case it is nearly always the daily psalms to which I turn), staying with the words, perhaps saying them out loud, trying to hear them as if for the first time. When I am arrested by something in particular, some small phrase, I read it time and time and time again. This is what the early Fathers liked to call chewing the cud, chewing it well so that it brings nourishment. I like to use analogies from my own life: rocking a small baby to sleep, or less romantically, watching the way in which clothes are swirled round and round when I switch on the washing machine. As I say it over and over again it becomes rather like a heartbeat, and that is the point at which I am moving on to the third stage, *oratio*. This is where the feelings and emotions come into play, carrying me beyond intellect and imagination. It is now as though I am at last allowing God to take charge, being open to him so that his love can grasp me, drag me to himself. Everything else falls away and instead I surrender totally to God. It is a pity to write too much about it, for it is essentially about love. It is as though we find ourselves becoming lost in the relationship with God; we are simply gazing at God, resting in him.[22]

Dom Columba Marmion, great Benedictine, drew all this together in a neat little exposition. We read, *lectio*, under the eye of God, *meditatio*, until the heart is touched, *oratio*, and leaps into flame, *contemplatio*. Guigo the Carthusian monk in a succession of questions gives us images for what happens:

> Do you not see how much juice has come from one little
> grape?
> Or how great a fire has been kindled from a spark?
> Or how this small piece of metal has acquired a new
> dimension by being hammered out on the anvil?

The word contemplation is in such wide use today that there is a real danger of it becoming fashionable and losing its substance. It is interesting to try to regain something of the fullness of the original meaning. The dictionary tells us that contemplation means 'to gaze attentively at something'. The root of the word is *templum*, a sacred space sectioned off or set apart for the priests, the augurs, to look 'inside animals, inside things', in order to find divine meanings and purpose. This I translate into my own terms as meaning to go deeply inside my own self in order to find the source and ground of my being. I am brought back to the idea of the attentiveness, vigilance, keeping watch, which marked the start of the monastic day and then continued to shape time. The Word is to be received into a reflective heart. Slowly, and with practice, this will become a state of being into which one is progressively immersed. *Memoria*, mindfulness, is the opposite of *oblivio*, heedlessness, the numbing of the mind, which of course includes those comfortable routines which can become evasions or escape routes.

Aelred spoke of clinging to God 'without any trace of forget-fulness', or, in another place, 'without any sense of weariness'. One of the favourite themes of Gilbert of Hoyland is the quiet mind, a mind in repose, free from useless activity, not entangled with preoccupations which unravel the spirit. He knew that the one essential thing was that the Word might be actualised in the life and experience of the monk, and that this meant mindfulness, the constant holding of Christ in the heart, 'stored in the memory, unfailing for your nourishment, abundant for your satisfaction'. A neat little Latin tag of William of St Thierry puts it well: *'ut agatur in nobis quod legitur in nobis*: that what we read about may be realised within us'.[23]

It was the Word that brought unity to the Cistercian experi-ence. Everything about the life was organised around this. The architecture itself, as we have seen, with its acoustical environment, was designed to give the Word its maximum impact. There was a continuity between the readings in the office, the reading aloud in the refectory during meals, and in private in *lectio divina*. Most of the manual work they did left them free to pray or to meditate in the silence of their hearts. In the rhythm of bringing to God the whole of one's self, body, mind and spirit, each activity flowed into the next, the one interpenetrating the other so powerfully that it became almost impossible to differentiate these degrees of varying intensity of contact with the Word. The Word heard in choir was carried always and everywhere. It was a well known dictum of Bernard that the soul meditating in the woods would learn from branches and boulders the hidden meanings of the Scriptures just as well as in the scriptorium.

So although in theory it might be possible to distinguish between different spiritual activities, and name them as reading, meditation, prayer or contemplation, in fact in prac-tice, the longer that the monk stayed with this life the less easy it became to make any sort of separation. The life was a unity which centred on Christ the Word.

The goal of this life is to be, to live, in Christ. Minds and hearts are formed by Christ, actions shaped by Christ. The monastery is a school in which to learn Christ. For what the Cistercian life shows us, as indeed is true of all Christian life, is that through the Word we encounter a person. Isaac of Stella ended a sermon:

> So, brothers, let Christ be your only master.
> Let him be for you a book written inside and out.
> In it read Christ.
> From it learn Christ.
> From this original make a copy of Christ
> both internally in your hearts
> and externally in your bodies.
> The others read in your life the manner of life that Christ
>   lived.
> This is why it is said [1 Corinthians 6:20]
> 'Glorify and carry God in your bodies.'
> May Christ himself be so kind as to give this gift.
> Amen.[24]

4. SIMPLICITY

The Spirit of Simplicity: Characteristic of the Cistercian Order is the title of the official Report produced by the general chapter in 1948, and dedicated to William of St Thierry on the 800th anniversary of his death. That succinct phrase sums up so clearly what has been emerging in these earlier pages: simplicity is the key to Cistercian life. The Cistercian ideal is one that emphasises utter simplicity and ordinariness. The life of the twelfth-century Cistercians guaranteed to those first monks 'all the lee-way and breathing-space of simplicity, that they might give themselves all of a piece to God' (words taken from the report).

As the monk learns to rid himself of what is unnecessary and superfluous he is the more able to enter into that interior simplicity. It is to escape from a world dominated by achievement and acquisition in all its many insidious forms. Chrysogonus Waddell makes this point in describing how his imaginary young novice Ernaut has left the University of Paris and in joining the community at Clairvaux discovers that it means entering into an economy of salvation both humble and humbling: 'a sacramental system involving the most ordinary materials, bread, wine, water, oil; Scriptures written in uncouth Latin compared to the Vergil or Horace he had studied at Paris; a chant that did not allow polyphony; field work and manual labour such as only serfs did'.[1] This is what Merton meant when he described monastic simplicity as being the 'concern with doing ordinary things quietly and perfectly for the glory of God, which is the beauty of pure Benedictine life, a beautiful and simple zeal, which was the very foundation stone of the Order'.

In 1948 Merton, comparatively new to monastic life but with the gift for languages, was put to translate the general chapter report. He was not entirely happy with it for he felt that it dealt with simplicity at the external levels of architecture, liturgy, clothing. So he added a long appendix, 'St Bernard on Interior Simplicity', in which he gives us a perceptive analysis of four of the most important Bernardine texts. The start must be interior simplicity: 'Seek him in the simplicity of your heart', for as Bernard tells us, this is demanded by the perfectly simple nature of God. The monk is a man of one-ness, simplicity: his very name says it, monachos: alone, single, simple.

Merton used a phrase that I particularly like when he said that the monk's wish was to give himself 'all of a piece to God'.[2] The second part of Merton's appendix appears under the title 'St Bernard on interior simplicity' in *Thomas Merton on St Bernard*. The lack of unity means being divided, torn apart by conflicting interests and appetites, which is dangerous not only for ourselves but for others too. Multiplicity, complexity are both contrary to monastic simplicity. No one can be at peace with their own selves, nor with one another, until they are at peace with God; this is the tranquillity of order on which everything else depends. *Tranquillus Deus tranquillat omnia.* Bernard sums it up simply in these few words: 'The tranquil God tranquillises everything in us'.[3]

William of St Thierry had expressed it so vividly in the passage quoted in the previous chapter: 'A man whose spirit is disordered is never alone, even when by himself, but is ever in the midst of a turbulent crowd.' A profound need for unity is something which we all recognise. One of the main reasons that brought Henri Nouwen to spend time at Genesee was exactly this. In his diary for 20 July, having been in the abbey a little over a fortnight, he wrote:

> Reflecting on my past three years of work I realise more and more that it lacked unity. The many things I did

during those years seem disjointed, not really relating to each other, not coming from one source. I prayed during certain hours or days but my prayer seemed separated from the lectures I gave, the trips I made, the counselling I did ... My fears and my resulting fatigue over the last three years might well be diagnosed as a lack of single-mindedess, as a lack of one-eyedness, *as a lack of simplicity* [my italics!]. Indeed, how divided my heart has been and still is! ... The characteristic of a saint is, to borrow Kierkegaard's words, 'To will one thing'. Well, I will more than one thing, am double-hearted, double-minded, and have a very divided loyalty.

In September, as he was still struggling with his divided self and his desire to be single-eyed and single-minded, he admitted that 'the simplicity that all this presupposes is not easy to attain. I find that my life constantly threatens to become complex and divisive. A life of prayer is basically a very simple life. This simplicity, however, is the result of asceticism and effort; it is not a spontaneous simplicity.' He goes on to say that his wish is to live a simple life so that preaching and teaching, lecturing and counselling could be like different forms of a meditative life. In other words he is looking for a centre from which everything can flow. He is honest enough to say rather wryly that he can see this clearly while he is in the abbey but he wonders if he will be able to hold on to it when he leaves and regains 'the fragmented and fragmenting world'.[4]

In the younger Thomas Merton whom we meet in the pages of his autobiography *The Seven Storey Mountain*, we see this same lack of unity, the wanderer endlessly searching for something new, trying new roles, new places, new experiences. His later writings allow us to watch the growth of a unitive simplicity, in which everything is held together and flows from one centre. He was never an artist, but he used the camera as a instrument of contemplation and his photographs tell us much about the way in which he saw the world.[5] When he was first lent a camera he showed an absorbing, almost childlike interest in it, and he had a very simple aim, to use it as a tool for 'dealing with things everybody knows about but isn't attentive to'. He had the gift of seeing through things into their centre. He quoted Maximus, the Greek father to whom he was greatly indebted, and from whom he learnt about the love of Christ hiding itself mysteriously in the inner nature of created things, so that in 'all that is varied lies hidden He who is One and eternally identical, in all composite things'. This was the message that he wanted to communicate to those whose eyes and hearts were open to receive it. 'Time and again he will say "It is all given" "Open your eyes and see" "Don't strive, wait attentively".' There is something almost Zen-like in his insistence on waiting for things to yield up their presences, rock, old fences, roots, whatever was actually there, right in front of his eyes:

> There is in all things
> an inexhaustible sweetness and purity,
> a silence that is a fount of action and joy.
> It rises up in wordless gentleness
> and flows out to me
> from the unseen roots of all created being,
> welcoming me tenderly,
> saluting me with indescribable humility.[6]

One of the things that helped Merton to see the world in these terms was the monastic understanding of detachment, which is perhaps better expressed in the word non-attachment. This means not wanting to possess or control, seeing the inner mystery of everything (and that of course includes persons), a standing back in order to let each thing be itself. In *The Silent Life* he wrote:

> As soon as we take them to ourselves,
> appropriate them,
> hug them to our hearts,

we have stolen them from God,
they are no longer His, but our own.[7]

To exercise possession is, in the monastic life, a sin against poverty. The Rule is quite adamant here: monks are to possess nothing of their own. Each is given what is necessary by the abbot so that no one lacks any of the essentials, but he must never regard these as his own personal property. At the first sign of any proprietorial ownership this vice is to be uprooted, amputated, pulled out by the roots. Benedict is quite clear: this is a serious vice and he attacks it as such. For what does the desire to possess, accumulate, do? It will fill up that inner void which keeps a person open to the experience of God.

It is not poverty per se that is important, but the spirit of poverty. There is nothing of dire poverty in the Benedictine or the Cistercian life. There is sufficiency but not superfluity; the care taken in the provision of food and the way in which it is served shows Benedict's respect and reverence for matter and material things. Food and clothing were based on the standards and practice of the farm labourers in the countryside around. The question asked of the visiting monk who wished to stay on at the monastery is revealing: is he content with what he found? Benedict repeats the word 'content' twice in this chapter, which is rather unusual for him, but it tells us how important he knows this to be. The example of the primitive community in Acts was always present in their minds. To share, to share gladly in the goods of this world, having all things in common and seeking to use them wisely, is to be open to the good of all. It is also a sign of being open to God; having nothing of one's own is to need others, and more than that, to need God.

Another example was that of the desert fathers and the apostles or St Paul. Benedict envisaged his monks living on the products of manual labour. 'Then only are they really monks if they live by the work of their hands, like our Fathers and the Apostles.' When the first Cistercians wished to return to the radical simplicity which they saw in the original concept of the Rule they recognised the role of manual labour as particularly important. For by the twelfth century the Benedictines seemed to have forgotten this – one historian claims to have found not a single reference to field or garden work being a 'common exercise' amongst them by this period.[8] A story is told of a man who had been a Benedictine monk for twenty years and then went to Clairvaux where he was astonished to see 'so many wise, noble and gently raised men' exerting themselves through the heat of the day to get in the harvest.

Here were men happy to accept poverty and rough clothing and obscurity, stripping themselves of proprietorship over everything that could stand between themselves and God. Refusing hired labour, they were proud that it was 'in the sweat of our brow, rather than that of servants or oxen, that we have to eat our bread', as Isaac of Stella put it in a sermon.[9] Nor did the presence of the lay brothers excuse the choir-monks from the ordinary daily manual work: *monachos laborando vivat*, and during harvest they were out at the granges helping in the fields with the harvest. André Louf, abbot of a monastery famous for its cheese, in writing of the place of work in a Cistercian community today, speaks of work as healing. He calls it 'a guarantee of normality' (when used in a sane and balanced fashion) and says that a question put to any aspirant, who might be led into a false spirituality far removed from the realities of everyday life, is 'What material do you work with?'

> Whatever it is – the soil, clay, wood, water, metal, cheese or chocolate, the monk needs this simple material to measure himself against, every day. He will thus be kept in contact with reality, for these things come from the hand of God and are solidly rooted in the earth from which they are drawn, and of which they remain a part.

He then goes on to quote a nice saying from Guerric of Igny: 'Work is a load by which, as ships are given weight so hearts are given quiet and gravity, and in it the outward man finds a firm foundation and a settled condition.'[10]

Work and prayer flowing one into another, body and soul joined harmoniously – here is the healing unity of the whole of one's person. The goal, again to quote from the Report, is 'the unification and simplification of the entire life of the monk, to produce in him the habit of *breathing God* in deep and continuous draughts in all simplicity, and with the dispositions of a child'.[11] This is of course nothing more or less than continual prayer, the most intimate and the most important part of the Cistercian life. It flows out of a life that is always at rest and yet never idle. Guerric of Igny concludes a sermon for the feast of the Assumption, speaking from his own experience: 'In all things therefore I have sought rest, even in work.' Here we are shown a mysterious truth, one which I see as amongst the most valuable gifts of the Cistercian way for today's world. It could hardly be more beautifully put than in this phrase of Bernard which I have already quoted earlier in this chapter: *Tranquillus Deus tranquillat omnia*: 'The tranquil God tranquillises everything' in us.

When Merton quoted this he commented on the way in which Cistercian simplicity is most perfectly expressed and fulfilled in a love for God which reduces everything to 'unity and peace in the tranquillity of contemplation in which the infinitely simple truth of God steeps our hearts in silence and joy'.[12]

An old monastic saying goes that you can tell how a man prays by the way in which he sweeps the cloister. There should be no dichotomy between the spiritual and the everyday reality of daily work. Nouwen was very resistant to this at first, and he is very honest and very amusing in telling how much he resented time spent in the bakery, on the hot bread line, or in the creek, pulling rocks out of the river for the new chapel, when he might be in the library reading about prayer, or better still, writing about prayer. He wondered how he could 'make my work more a part of my prayer and not just an occasion to fret', and talking about this with the abbot, John Eudes Bamberger, he was astonished to discover that the monks, especially the older ones, really enjoyed manual work, and this encouraged him to continue to struggle to learn to make the work of his hands also into prayer. But later, as the unity of the monastic life began to take hold, he came to realise that manual work as much as the liturgy and spiritual reading were all essential aspects of prayer. 'How can manual work be prayer? It is prayer when we not only work with our hands but also with our hearts . . . when manual work no longer leads us to God, we are no longer fully realising our vocation to pray without ceasing.'[13]

But work has another aspect which André Louf brings out by reminding us that in the book of Genesis we are told how God cursed the earth and work was imposed on Adam and Eve so that the earth might bring forth the fruits they needed in order to live. Work is a part of the suffering which invaded the world after sin. Work is therefore marked with a double sign. It has its harsh side, and it is important to recognise this. Anyone who lives close to the earth and to the round of seasonal activity on the land cannot be romantic about it. There is the cutting into and cutting back, often in an almost cruel way: cutting deep furrows into the soil; slicing away at new growth on fruit trees; cutting the young growth in a copse; shearing sheep. Addressing those with pastoral responsibilities in the community, John of Forde, living in that lovely stretch of countryside between Dorset and Somerset, knew the connection between shearing and fruitfulness:

> If anyone desires to shear me into poverty and patience so that I may learn from him to become poor and naked . . . then he must first practice what he is preaching. If he is to shear without hindrance, then first let him be sheared himself.[14]

The paring away of what is unnecessary brings up the question of asceticism, a word not much in favour today. Yet it formed an essential part of the wholeness of the Cistercian life. In its root it simply means training, exercise. It was accepted in the early centuries without question, for it was seen as integral to monastic life. The extravagances of some of the later mortifications, which tended to become prodigious feats of spiritual athleticism, may have given examples which many of us find extremely distasteful. However, when I read what Basil Pennington tells me about what self-denial means in his own Cistercian experience, I find it put into context:

> I do not think we will handle these [i.e., human conflicts and things going wrong in daily life] well and sanctify them and make them efficacious by offering them in union with Christ's passion if we do not prize the worth of penance and self-denial. When we do truly prize the worth of suffering and the cross in the Christ plan, then it is inevitable that we are not content solely with what happens to come along in the course of our daily living and labor. We want to do more and seek to do more. As St Benedict says, we come to love fasting (no matter how much we love feasting) and watching (no matter how much we love the pillow) and all the other exercises of the monastic life.[15]

The serious attention paid by the Cistercian tradition to asceticism is one of its distinguishing marks. Its purpose is transfiguration. It has nothing to do with the prowess or the ability of the individual – it is being open to grace, to the exercise of grace at work, transforming, bringing life out of death, the new out of the old.

This question of asceticism brings us again to the subject of silence and the creative role that it plays in the Cistercian life. I have found what André Louf says about this very helpful:

> The asceticism of silence should create a silence, an emptiness in the depths of the being where God can be heard without any other noise. Silence imposes itself on us inwardly in two ways. It issues from our poverty and it springs from our plenitude ... Silence wells up from an emptiness within us, but it is an emptiness freely and fully accepted ... A moment comes when silence alone can express the extraordinary richness in our heart. Such a

silence enfolds a person gently and powerfully and always comes from within . . . It establishes a zone of peace and quiet around the one who is silent, where God can be irresistibly felt as present.[16]

I am brought back again to the image of the inner cloister, that place of emptiness to be filled with God, that bareness and simplicity that gives the context for everything else that will flow out from that centre.

5. INTEGRATION

'Know, my brothers, that in this life it is necessary never to separate these two women.' On the feast of the Assumption, the Cistercian patronal festival, the gospel passage set for the day was Luke 10:42, the story of Mary and Martha in the house at Bethany, which inevitably became the subject of many sermons. Aelred told his brothers:

> You see, if Mary had been alone in the house, no one would have fed the Lord; if Martha had been alone, no one would have tasted his presence and his words. Martha thus represents the action, the labour accomplished for Christ, Mary the repose that frees from bodily labour, in order to taste the sweetness of the Lord in reading, prayer, and contemplation. That is why, my brothers, so long as Christ is on earth, poor, subject to hunger, to thirst, to temptation, it is necessary that these two women inhabit the same house, that in one soul the two activities occur . . .

Then he goes on to speak of the implications for his hearers, who would of course on this occasion be the entire community, the choir-monks together with the hundreds of lay brothers coming in from the furthest granges:

> Do not neglect Mary for Martha,
> nor Martha for Mary.
> If you neglect Martha, who will serve Jesus?
> And if you neglect Mary,
> what will be the use of the visit of Jesus,

since you will not taste his sweetness?
Know, my brothers, that in this life it is necessary
never to separate these two women.[1]

From its earliest days the Cistercian Order found itself
asking how it might combine the call to the desert, the need
for solitude and silence, with the demands of loving and
serving others. How can these two lives be reconciled? Is it
possible to combine action and contemplation? It remains of
course a perennial question and I have found it illuminating
to turn to these men who struggled with it with great honesty.
The problem was not of course anything new in monastic
experience. Even Antony himself, father of monks, had found
that people came to seek him out in his solitude in the desert
and the pattern of life was one of engagement and withdrawal.
The holy man became the destination for pilgrims and for
those in search of a healer and wonder-worker, with the nice
irony, as Peter Brown remarked, that 'the lonely cells of the
recluses of Egypt have been revealed by the archaeologists to
have been well furnished consulting rooms'.[2]

Bernard himself knew both the world and the cloister, and
in his life tried to balance both elements – however painful
that might be. He writes of the experience of being snatched
from a moment of union with God in contemplation through
the necessity of serving his neighbour. His conviction was that
every true contemplative will prove the authenticity of his or
her experience of God by the alacrity with which they submit
to the constraints of the call of charity. For he spent half
his time outside the monastery, involved with political and
ecclesiastical affairs which he saw as necessities thrust upon
him by what he felt to be his obligations to the world outside.
He became one of the strongest powers of his day, the arbiter
of Europe, politician, statesman, intervening with a zeal that
sometimes seemed to verge on excess. Bernard found his
inspiration above all in the Beatitudes. Charles Dumont makes
this fascinating parallel between Bernard and Dietrich Bonho-
effer, who in this century tried to come to grips with the

half-hearted formalism of a church which he found devoid of
spiritual vitality. 'I believe that I cannot have interior honesty
and integrity unless I begin to take seriously the Sermon on
the Mount. This is the only source of energy . . .'[3]

Yet writing to a canon regular called Oger, who had resigned
his superiorship in order to return to the obscurity of the
common life, Bernard rebuked him for a defection from duty.
'Your repose has pleased you more than outside usefulness.'
He called this a false humility, for he had resisted the *ordinatio
caritatis* on which true sanctity depends. The actual letter is
stern:

> I congratulate you that you have unburdened yourself,
> but I am afraid that you have dishonoured God, in so far
> as you can. You have doubtless resisted his ordering of
> things when you cast yourself down after being promoted
> by him . . . There is nothing haughtier than this, for you
> have preferred your own counsel to God's, choosing to be
> at rest for your own sake rather than to do his work, to
> which he had taken you up.[4]

Bishops were often chosen from Cistercian communities and
while Bernard said they should be revered, he warned against
any envy of their apostolate or their dignity, entered upon only
as a special mission from God, a mission made known through
obedience through the interior inspiration of grace.

His letter to his protégé Eugenius, the first Cistercian pope
to ascend the throne of Peter, shows that he understood the
demands of a life of public responsibility in the Church only
too well. His first anxiety was that Eugenius' interior life was
barely sufficient to cope with this vocation, so he urged on him
the practice of meditation and other exercises, in clear and
definite injunctions: 'Do not give yourself entirely to activity,
and do not engage in active works all the time. Keep something
of your heart and of your time, for meditation!' But while he
says that it would be far more desirable if Eugenius could give
himself much more time for prayer since the life of prayer
should always, if possible, prevail over activity, he remains a

realist. In an active life, prayer and meditation, the consideration of divine things, should always exercise the greatest attraction on our hearts, so that even in our activity we long to return to them. He warned him of the dangers of the papal machine in salutary words which could well be put above the desk of anyone exercising authority in the Church today:

> Where shall I begin? Let me begin with the pressure of business. If you hate it, I sympathise with you. If you do not, I mourn all the more, because the unconscious patient is in the greater danger ... See where all this damnable business is leading you! You are wasting your time ... What fruit is there in these things? They can only create cobwebs.[5]

Yet Bernard can be splendidly down to earth in taking to task monks who felt superior because of their own contemplative life. For a contemplative religious to find fault with those engaged in a far more difficult and dangerous vocation is like a woman who is sitting and sewing in a window-seat and criticising the soldiers of a returning army.

> A woman at home spinning rashly reprimands her husband returning from battle. And I tell you: if someone in the cloister happens to notice that a prelate working among the people handles himself with less constraint than he himself does, and with less circumspection – for example, in speaking, eating, sleeping, laughing, getting angry, passing judgement – let him not leap to pass judgement precipitately.[6]

There are of course a few who are set apart for the contemplative life, and called to leave the world, as the anchorite to whom Aelred wrote, 'This is your portion, dearly beloved. Dead and buried to the world, you should be deaf to all that belongs to the world and unable to speak of it.' But this is an exceptional vocation and for the most part people must live the mixed life in the world and try to hold action and contemplation in balance. So even though contemplation is in itself

superior and preferable to action, and in so far as we are free
to do so we must seek it, in practice we are often bound to
give first place to that which has a more immediate claim upon
our attention. The contemplative must yield to active love
when it is required. Aelred took the story of Jesus at the age
of twelve having to leave the spiritual delights of Jerusalem
in order to return to Nazareth with his parents as an example
of how contemplatives must 'put the needs of those in their
care before the delights of contemplation'.[7] In another sermon
he made this same point, that without the active life contemplation cannot lead anyone to perfection.

> All our good works consist in two things,
> namely in the active and the contemplative life.
> The active life is like wool clothing;
> the contemplative life is like linen clothing.
> the former is rougher, the latter more comfortable;
> the former exterior, the latter interior.
> The active life can indeed suffice against the coldness of
>   damnation
> and can wipe away all the shamefulness of sins;
> without the active life, the contemplative life cannot,
> in this mortal domain, lead anyone to perfection.[8]

One of Bernard's favourite words was *alternatio*, alternation,
the ideal of the harmonious holding together in balance. He
has some moving passages in which he speaks of how this
mixed life will flow from the superabundance of contemplation.
It is the call to pass beyond contemplation to the care of souls.
He speaks of it in terms of marriage, the mystical marriage
which is not sterile but will bring forth children. I find myself
comforted when he confesses how difficult this can be. 'In the
midst of these alternations the mind vacillates, fearful and
greatly agitated lest perhaps it cling more than it should to
one of them . . .' The answer, as he reminds us (in Sermon 18
on the Song of Songs), is that this is a special gift from God;
it is the operation of the Holy Spirit.

It is good to return to the image of Mary and Martha. I find that it is concrete, vivid and manageable, an image to which I can relate when more abstract ideas become rather threatening. Here are two women, two friends; they live together in one house, under one roof. They support one another, they complete one another. They are sisters, not enemies. Jesus needed both. And then I see how this applies to me, how Jesus needs to find both Mary and Martha in my own self. Aelred puts it so simply:

> It must be remembered
> that Martha laboured
> and Mary was free from work
> in the same house;
> in the same soul in whom Christ is welcomed,
> both lives are led,
> each in its own time, place and order.[9]

But how do I harmonise Mary and Martha in myself? This is urgent since unless I do there will be this terrible split, which can be so exhausting and debilitating, as I feel myself being pulled in different directions. The key lies in that final word order. As soon as I see that Bernard is telling me that contemplation is, in itself, superior and preferable to action, but on the other hand action is often 'better' or 'more necessary' than contemplation, I am freed of that guilt which tells me that one or the other is right. Instead it is the interplay or interchange between them which is creative of 'the order of love' – the two orders of love which must coexist together here below.

A perfection that ends in ourselves, that does not 'contribute to the growth of the whole Christ', in the uncompromising words of Merton, is not Christian sanctity. This is the end for which the two lives are held together. In the Stoic view, as Seneca had noted, it was necessary to live according to both action and contemplation, but the guiding principle in this case was that of personal inner tranquillity. Instead the guiding principle for the Christian is love. Here is the basis for action, the corrective to guard us against rushing into any ill-considered activity. In order to be able to give fully and appropriately to others we must take in, receive, ponder in meditation what God wants for them. This is only possible in the context of love. God's activity in us, which Bernard calls infusion, must come first, and then effusion – activity flowing from love – will become profitable, as he says in his eighteenth sermon on the Canticle.

> Why, if you are wise,
> will you be a reservoir and not a canal?
> Because at one and the same time the canal pours out
> what it receives,
> but the reservoir retains the water
> till it is full
> and then communicates the overflow
> without damage to itself or disadvantage . . .[10]

'The psaltery should be enjoyed with the lute, nor is the sound of the lute less enjoyable than that of the psaltery, although it produces its sound from the bottom and the other does it from the top.' Those who travel by these various ways are all travelling to God. *Ad idem tendunt, licet non eadem via*: 'They tend to the same end, although not by the same route.' The lay brothers listening to the message of the Gospel on their patronal festival could never have felt themselves inferior, for they knew the work of Martha was as vital as the prayer of Mary – Christ needed both, for in the end both grew out of the order of love.

6. GROWTH

Looking around his own monastery Bernard must have seen that the beauty of its life lay in its diversity, that those who entered were not all poured into one mould so that they would emerge with the same identical form. His neat little Latin tag, which ended the previous chapter, *Ad idem tendunt, licet non eadam via*, 'those who travel by these various ways are all travelling to God', makes the point. He accepted the pluralism of function of the different orders within the Church: 'All contribute to the perfection of the saints, and all press on together toward mature manhood, according to the measure of the age of Christ's fullness.' There is no one single pattern, no single experience: instead God acts variously within the life of each individual. Each person finds his or her own secret way. All that is asked of us is that we should remain open to the formative influence of grace, so that there may be a constant development of the spirit, a progressive growth into the 'Christ-life'.

Bernard, like Benedict, is concerned with progress. The language of the Rule is dynamic: to return, to run, to progress, to look towards the end, the goal. But in spite of this urgency the message is also that we each of us go at our own pace, not under pressure. 'Let change come quietly and invisibly' wrote Merton in May 1968, in the last year of his life.[1] In an age in which there is so much writing about the techniques of the inner life, presenting us with differing types of spirituality, all competing in the market place, it is a relief to find the Cistercians making no such claims. Nowhere, they remind us, is there anything that imposes system on the inner life, or brings dependence on a method, which is something I find very freeing. 'You will please him more speedily if you keep to your own level and do not seek things which are above you.' The Cistercian Fathers are always reminding us that we are not in control, that the initiative lies with God and our lives are not a matter of human planning but of adaptability in the hands of God. There is only one thing, however, which is necessary, and that is to keep guard over our hearts and over our understanding, and thus to remain sensitive and responsive to the workings of the Spirit. Vigilance is important, for the time appropriate for one thing may not be appropriate for another.

The Spirit leaves us from time to time, in order that we may seek him more urgently. How will this happen if we do not even notice his departure? The dialectic of presence and absence is an important theme in the Song of Songs, as in any love affair. Above all we should be aware that the Spirit comes and goes, so that we reverence and obey him when he is there, and experience the desire for him when he is absent. The visitations of the Word to the soul are fleeting, sudden, very temporary indeed. 'Just as one thought to hold onto him, he slipped away . . . he allows himself to be touched, but not clung to, for just as suddenly he again eludes the grasp.' It was Bernard's firm teaching that the alternation between positive and negative experience is a universal law of spiritual growth; he was suspicious of an even life, as unauthentic and subject to substantial delusion.

I am reassured by this, by someone who knows what most of us experience, namely the dual stream by which there are times of pleasure and relief and also of darkness and heaviness. There is not even any question of falling and failing – it is only to be expected. I should be aware that the love of God will be received and reciprocated in different ways throughout my life. Again and again the theme is 'good and appropriate' to where I am. At times I need to be comforted, at times challenged. We are all under mercy and under judgement. There is consolation and there is also correction. We have to attend to both. Each is relevant and each is important. If we cling too much to mercy then there is the danger of becoming 'slack, negligent, tepid in prayer, slothful in deed'. But on the other hand if we cling to judgement then we shall be 'cast down by an unbelievable fear and by misery and confusion, surrounded on all sides by a terrifying darkness'. Bernard therefore concludes 'since I have been instructed by the experience of my master [i.e. the Psalmist] it is not judgement alone or mercy alone, but both together which will be my song'.[2]

Our earthly life is one of seeking, of seeking the God who is seeking us. That is the question that the novice entering the community is asked: Are you truly seeking God? Bernard tells us that God should be sought sincerely, frequently and perseveringly; that he should be sought by desires and deeds. But this is only part of the story. God is in the seeking business first. The Lord is looking for his workman. So the search is a response. Bernard says we seek because we have been found, found out, called. 'Meanwhile, I will seek you, Lord, by loving you, for he who loves you seeks you, since to find you is to love you with a perfect love.' Aelred, in a passage from the first page of *The Mirror of Charity*, is speaking of how we sigh on our pilgrimage, the hunger and thirst which are a foretaste of what will be revealed. The ardent and persevering desire for God is a gift of the seeking God to the one who is seeking him. Early Cistercian life was not oriented towards prayer in general, nor towards the office in particular, but simply towards God.[3]

> I seek your face,
> by your own gift I seek your countenance . . .
> I know indeed and I am sure
> that those who walk
> in the light of your countenance
> do not fall but walk in safety . . .[4]

These lines are taken from the third of William of St Thierry's *Meditations* or soliloquies which he considered apt 'for forming novices' minds to prayer'. He writes of a way of light, filled with illuminating graces, since he wishes for his followers what he has himself found, a path illumined by the face of God. Here is the call to transforming union set out directly. He invites his disciples to begin with meditation on the human life of Christ, and then through the passion they will come into contact with the depths of love that that reveals. Love calls forth love and the love called forth transforms the lover into the likeness of the beloved, a likeness which changes communion into union with God. William is showing me the fullest and richest meaning of Christian life in terms which I find I can enter into, for here I am given truth at once ultimate and yet accessible. I now see why so often in early Cistercian writing there is so much on the humanity of Christ, from that tiny vulnerable baby in swaddling clothes in a crib through every stage of his life on earth, and not least his sufferings on the cross.

This love affair does not develop in a vacuum. William describes how the monastic way is there to create a climate favourable to fostering its growth, with obedience as an essential element. 'The labour of obedience', as Benedict so realistically called it, is important for anyone, but especially important for those who are newly on the way. William has the Lord address these words to the beginner:

> I will go before you,
> and you must follow as you see me go before.
> I endured and laboured
> and you must labour too. I suffered many things,
> it behoves you, too, to suffer some.
> Obedience is the way to charity,
> and you will get there if you keep to it.[5]

The vow of *conversatio morum*, of conversion (metanoia, turning round, moving forward, journeying on), is of course one of the Cistercian vows taken over from the Rule of Benedict, together with obedience and stability. The idea of the journey is one of the inescapable themes of monastic life, as it must be of any human experience. But it is good to be reminded that this is not always a journey in which we move forward, in a straight line, but one in which, as Gilbert of Hoyland says here, we may find ourselves retracing, learning to see in a different way:

> Good is the journey
> when forgetting what lies behind,
> one presses on to what lies ahead
> in the hope of somehow reaching one's goal.
> Good assuredly is the journey
> not only whenever new and more hidden truths are
>   grasped
> but also when truths already grasped are unfolded
> with an affection
> ever new and ever fresh,
> not only when one covers new ground,
> but when one frequently retraces ground already
>   covered.
> Delightful then is the journey . . .[6]

'The Story of the King's Son' is the first of a series of eight parables that are now considered to be authentic compositions by Bernard. They make most enjoyable reading, imaginative and entertaining, with a wealth of colourful detail and an accomplished sense of storytelling. Time and again I have found myself being reminded of Bunyan's *Pilgrim's Progress*:

> And lo, Fortitude, the Lord's military champion appeared. He surged through the fields of Boldness, wielding the sword that is Joy. 'Do not be disturbed' he cried, 'there are more for us than for them.' But Prudence, the seasoned counsellor of the heavenly court replied: 'Please be careful . . . Let us advance prudently and without haste.'

In a final paragraph Bernard reveals his purpose. He tells his readers that 'there are four stages to be noted in the boy's return to freedom', and explains that the significance of 'the flight, rash and unthinking', for example, or 'the battle terrible and frightening' is to show us that they are phases through which all must pass. Michael Casey, who has translated these parables and made them available to us, tells us that they are 'intended to be a description of the process by which a monk makes his way to the freedom for which he was created. What we have here is a phenomenology of growth.' We watch the king's son, at first weak and silly, then with better times becoming precipitate and rash; when troubles come, losing heart and growing fearful, but finally, 'when they arrive at the kingdom of Charity, they are far-seeing, experienced and made perfect'. The description of the battle is a splendid piece of writing: the violent and unseen attack from the enemy, the city overwhelmed, the walls breached, ambushes planned and firebrands thrown, as the enemy presses in on every side, bringing fear and anguish. It is in this desperate extremity that God finally acts. Bernard's choice of the image of the battle for the human soul, and the message that the progress towards heaven is a sustained struggle, was well chosen since he was addressing young men who had probably left a knightly estate in order to enter the monastery. Michael Casey comments: 'Bernard is perhaps warning the young monks who form his audience against being surprised by the struggles that lie ahead of them . . . There are many defeats to be faced before the final victory is given.'[7]

One of the attractions that I have found in Cistercian writings is that while they do not set out any single itinerary of spiritual progress, they do yet manage to present me with stages, or perhaps I should think of them more as waymarks or pointers, for my journey. They should certainly not be taken as descriptions for the actual journey itself since that is always going to be unique, conducted at the discretion of the Holy Spirit. Many of us today when we think of the stages of spiritual growth are likely to think first of the three stages described by St John of the Cross: purgative, illuminative, unitive. In the Cistercian fathers we find many divisions: four degrees of love; seven progressive states of grace that culminate in the fullness of love; the eight Beatitudes as a model for leading a person step by step; there are twelve steps in the progress of humility. Three is inevitably used because of the three persons of the Trinity at work in us. Bernard has the three ointments of the Bride, contrition, devotion and piety, and these are seen in ascending order as applied to the feet, head, and whole Body of Christ, that is, the Church. But there are also the three kisses: only after the preparatory kisses of the feet (the penitential preparation) and the kiss of the hands (the practice of virtue) is the soul ready for the kiss of the mouth, or the direct encounter. This is developed in the first twelve sermons on the Song of Songs, the book to which he, like so many others in the Middle Ages, turned to find the source for the traditional mystical interpretation of the relationship between the soul and God. Here we are given the language of the bedchamber, the kiss, the lover and the beloved, love as desire. The Song of Songs is a poetic dialogue between the bride and the bridegroom, which can be interpreted as the drama of salvation at two levels, for the bride represents both the Church and also the soul. The drama opens in the middle of a conversation: 'Let him kiss me with the kiss of his mouth'. The speaker is the bride sighing with longing for her lover. It leads on to the chamber of the king where the soul 'rests secretly in the king's embrace. While in this chamber the soul sees things that the human eye cannot see and hears mysteries that no tongue can repeat . . .'

Of course the way will be hard and rugged, and there will be times of boredom and heaviness and weariness. All the Cistercian fathers were quite honest about that. But they tried to keep their eyes and their thoughts fixed on the horizon. Bernard called his monks 'those who run toward joy', hastening in joy towards their heavenly homeland. It was said of the early Cistercians that, like the saints, their faces 'shone with joy, they had the face of one going towards Jerusalem'. *O quam felix*, Abbot Pierre, the twelfth-century Abbot of Igny, was to be heard repeating frequently: 'How happy I am with God'; and *O felix* is a favourite formula in almost every sermon of Gilbert of Hoyland.

When his own brother was on his death bed the monks

hurried to find Bernard in the middle of the night, exclaiming
with astonishment 'He is going, and singing for joy.' Bernard
arrived just in time to find Gerard finishing the last verse of
Psalm 148, his face alight with overflowing joy, and even in
his grief at the death of his own brother he could not forget
Gerard's joy at going home to his fatherland. But then he
habitually combined the theme of the journey in this life with
looking towards the heavenly Jerusalem, the city of God, the
homeland towards which we are travelling, the place in which
our longings will be satisfied:

> The deep happiness of the heavenly homeland
> for which our earthly pilgrimage continues to sigh,
> transcends not only every human sense,
> but also the understanding of the heart ...
> A place of delights,
> where the just are given to drink from the river of
> delights.
> A place of splendour,
> where the just shine forth with all the brilliance of the
> night sky.
> A place of happiness,
> where eternal joy is on their heads.
> A place of plenty,
> where nothing is wanting to those who see him.
> A place of sweetness, where the Lord sweetly makes his
> presence known to all.
> A place of vision, where a great sight is seen.[8]

Here Bernard gives us one of his most beautiful assertions
about heaven, gentle and poetic, infused with a sense of light:

> O true noon-day
> when warmth and light are at their peak
> and the sun at its zenith
> and no shadows fall;
> when stagnant waters dry up
> and their fetid odours disperse.

O never ending solstice
when daylight lasts forever.
O noon-day light,
marked with the mildness of spring,
stamped with summer's bold beauty,
enriched with autumn's fruit,
and (lest I seem to forget)
calm with winter's rest from toil.

'Happy are you if your gaze is fixed in him.' Their gaze was on
heaven but it was equally on the figure of Jesus Christ himself.
In the pattern of the liturgical year they would find themselves
living out the pattern of Christ's own life, following it step by
step and applying its mysteries to their own lives. Every abbot
would have to preach to the entire community fifteen times
a year on major liturgical feasts. So Bernard speaks of 'the
sacrament of Advent', the start of that journey by which they
will follow Jesus through his passion and to his ascension. It is
also of course a movement from darkness to light, and Merton,
entering Gethsemani on 10 December 1941, realised how
important it was that this, the start of his new life when he
had at last come home after those years of fruitless wandering,
should be at the beginning of the liturgical year.

> Liturgically speaking you could hardly find a better time
> to become a monk than Advent. You begin a new life, you
> enter into a new world at the beginning of a liturgical
> year. And everything that the Church gives you to sing,
> every prayer that you say in and with Christ in his Mys-
> tical Body is a cry of ardent desire for grace, for help, for
> the coming of the Messiah, the Redeemer. The soul of the
> monk is a Bethlehem where Christ comes to be born . . .
>
> It is a desire all the more powerful, in the spiritual
> order, because the world around you is dead. Life has
> ebbed to its dregs. The trees are stripped bare. The birds
> forget to sing. The grass is brown and grey. You go out to
> the fields with mattocks to dig up the briars.[9]

It was the more powerful for Merton since this was his first encounter with Gregorian chant, with what he called its austere warmth. He sees how its measured tone takes the old words and infuses into them even more strength and conviction and meaning. He enters into the singing of the traditional Advent hymns, many of them dating from the early years of the Church, and finds in them a simplicity, balance and strength unlike anything that he had found in secular music. During that first year he found that the feasts and seasons of the liturgical year, and the various times of sowing and planting and harvesting, together began to fill up his life and to make of it one whole: a closely integrated harmony of natural and supernatural cycles. By the time that it was once again Christmas he found that it brought the same kind of grace and consolation, only more intense. He was making an important discovery about what it meant to enter into the pattern of a monastic year.

When Bernard would recall his community to the major events of Christ's life, it was to take them beyond the outward form to their inner meaning, a sharing in the mysteries of his life. So this is not some form of pious recollection but rather a reminder of God's love as we watch Christ from his birth in the manger, through all the events of his life of prayer and preaching, suffering and death, resurrection and ascension.

> He was incomprehensible and inaccessible,
> invisible and completely unthinkable.
> Now he wishes to be comprehended,
> wishes to be seen,
> wishes to be thought about.
> How, do you ask?
> As lying in the manger,
> resting in the Virgin's lap,
> preaching on the mountain,
> praying through the night,
> or hanging on the cross,
> growing pale in death,

free among the dead and ruling in hell,
and also as rising on the third day,
showing the apostles the place of the nails,
the signs of victory,
and finally as ascending over heaven's secrets in their
   sight.[10]

Bernard sums up the whole programme of life in Christ with a short formula: 'Conform yourself to the Son of Man'. One of the reasons for the mystery of the incarnation was to leave us an example so that we might follow in his footsteps:

> Our Lord and Saviour Jesus Christ, wishing to show us how we might ascend to heaven, did himself what he wished to teach . . . Since he would not ascend before first of all descending . . . he took to himself our nature . . .

So Christ imitated our human condition and Bernard next asks:

> What is the reason for this, brothers? What need was there for the Lord of Majesty to empty himself, to humiliate himself, to make himself little, unless it be that you might do the same? He already proclaims by his example what he will later preach in word: 'Learn from me, for I am gentle and humble in heart' . . . Do not allow such a valuable example to have been given to you in vain; but rather, conform yourselves to this model and be renewed even to the intimate depths of your being.[11]

Christ's human experience included destitution, misery. Bernard in one of his sermons spoke of 'all the anxious hours and bitter experiences of my Lord', which he carries round with him, like a little bunch of myrrh placed between his breasts:

> First from the privations of his infancy,
> then from the hardships he endured in preaching,
> the fatigues of his journeys,
> the long watches in prayer,

> the temptations when he fasted,
> his tears of compassion,
> the heckling when he addressed the people,
> and finally the dangers from traitors in the brotherhood,
> the insults,
> the spitting,
> the blows,
> the mockery,
> the scorn,
> the nails and similar torments that are multiplied in the
>   Gospels
> and all for the salvation of our race.[12]

The monk is formed, nourished and renewed by contemplation on the passion, on the wood of the cross, on the crown of thorns, which become most dear to him. Here Gilbert of Hoyland with great gentleness and tenderness shows us what it means to him:

> The softest of pillows for me, good Jesus,
> is that crown of thorns from your head.
> A welcome little bed is that wood of your Cross.
> On this I am bred and born,
> created and re-created
> and upon the altars of your passion
> I gladly rebuild for myself
> the nest of memory.[13]

If the monk wants to be constantly mindful of Christ then he must be willing to retrace the footsteps of Christ in his passion. These words of Gilbert of Hoyland seem a spontaneous outpouring of prayer which he wished his hearers to share in, keeping their eyes, as he does, on Christ.

> Noble is the path which your Beloved trod before you.
> Holy indeed is the ascent you prepare for yourself.
> Climb these steps barefoot and unshod.
> Here gladly set your foot
> that your foot may be dyed in the blood of Christ.

With this blood
dye not only your foot,
but also your hand and your head,
that you may ascend wholly purple,
wholly royal and wholly ennobled
by the passion of Christ.
If you share his passion you share his kingdom.[14]

This devotion to the sacred humanity of Christ, to the nativity as well as the passion, is just the beginning of the itinerary that will lead on to spiritual love. This transition can be seen as a form of imitation of Christ, which is why the resurrection and even more the ascension were so special for the early Cistercians. If we have followed the Christ who has come down to earth it will be even greater joy, at the end of time, to know him in heaven. By following the liturgical cycle up to the ascension it becomes possible to pray 'Draw me after you', in the words of the bride in the Song of Songs. On the feast of the Assumption, with the thought of our Lady caught up into heaven, Aelred tells his listeners that joy awaits us all at the end of our journey:

It is a great joy to consider how our Lord lay in a manger,
but it is a far greater joy to contemplate how he reigns
    in heaven.
It is a great joy to consider how he nursed at his mother's
    breasts,
but it is a far greater joy to contemplate how he feeds all
    creation.
It is a great joy to consider him in the arms of one
    maiden,
but it is a far greater joy to contemplate how he holds
within himself everything in heaven and on earth.[15]

7. LOVE AND KNOWLEDGE

> Our vocation is . . .
> above all to keep to that more excellent way
> which is the way of love,
> to advance day by day in these things
> and persevere in them until the last day.

These words from a letter that Bernard wrote to the monks of
the Abbey of Saint John in the Alps give a perfect summary
of what lies at the heart of Cistercian spirituality. The end of
life is love. It is as simple as that. Their foundation document,
The Charter of Charity, makes this clear for it had declared
that the purpose of their life was 'wholly ordered to love . . .
lived with a certain intensity to foster our growth in love', as
a monk following the Cistercian vocation today puts it.[1]

In attempting to follow the Rule in its integrity those first
Cistercian fathers wanted to recover the fullness of Benedict's
understanding of love. The mystic union with God in love was
the end of the monastic life as they understood it. The Rule
has no end: that final chapter points beyond itself. Benedict
called the monastery a school of love, the place in which the
novice comes to experience a real knowledge, a deep appreci-
ation, of his own self as loved with a love that is a reflection
of the love of God for each one made in his own image. Gradually he becomes more capable of loving, with a love which is
strong, gentle and humble. Benedict had made it clear: the
monk loves his abbot, his spiritual father, the exemplar of
Christ to the brothers, with humble affection, *humilis caritas*.

The visiting monk is expected to make any comments 'with the humility of love'.

Chapter Seven of the Rule, the twelve steps of humility, has always been considered the heart and centre of the Benedictine ascesis. The central place given by Benedict to humility ensured that the monk has to face with honesty the reality of being earthed in the knowledge of the real self. As André Louf reminds us, humility means at once true and near the ground, *humus*: 'Only the one who touches rock-bottom, the ground of his being and of his deepest feelings, can be spontaneously and deeply true, and truly humble.'[2]

It says something about the sureness of Bernard's insight into the meaning of the Cistercian vocation that his first treatise is concerned with humility, and it tells us something too of the spirit with which he approached the way of Benedict: he sees that the whole value of the ladder lies in its ability to bring us to the way of truth. When he wrote *The Steps of Humility* Bernard had been an abbot for about ten years, carrying the weighty responsibility of caring for his rapidly growing community. He was a good teacher. Before constructing his steps he arouses our interest by showing us the heights to which they can lead.[3] And that is truth. Not simply a moral sense or a quality of mind, but the incarnate Word, God himself known and contemplated. For Bernard there are three steps or degrees of humility, humility, love and contemplation. These correspond to the three degrees of the perception of truth, the truth in oneself, the truth in one's neighbour, and Truth itself. He makes the distinction between the humility which is striven for externally, and the humility of heart, which for him is the truth. The final step of Benedict's ladder of twelve steps brings the monk to the place where he can say, in the prayer of the publican or the words of the psalms, 'I am bowed down and humbled in every way' (*Rule*, 7.65–6).

The publican stands way down in the last place, the place of his own weakness. He knows this weakness and accepts it, and even is to some extent reconciled to it – though at the same time he cries out to God from the depths of his heart. He is the one who touches rock bottom, the ground of his being, his deepest feelings, so that he is spontaneously and deeply true, and truly humble. In the Pharisee we see the contrast: the well meaning, but purely human striving for perfection. The perfection ideal, with all its many images of climbing to the mountain top, succeeding in some heroic undertaking, was probably one which the young novice would bring with him into the community, just as it is for most of us something encouraged by the success-oriented world we live in, with its expectations of achievement. This pressure to succeed, this ego-ideal, may well also be something rooted in our unconscious, whether it comes from a need for love or security, or perhaps from the ever-present father as an authority figure. To live from some ideal of perfection, whether imposed internally or externally, or to be subject to some form of legalistic piety, has many dangers, as we know only too well. It often means living off fear or acting out fear-inspired behaviour patterns and obligations. It does not pay any dividends in the long run except in terms of anxiety, tension, loss of freedom.

Instead only when I admit my weakness, admit my need for help, can I even begin this extraordinary process which is to ascend descending. To be brought to zero point means giving up the false self. It may be that it is only some sort of crisis, loss or bereavement in all the many forms that takes (of which death is only one form and sometimes comparatively straightforward), that we are given the opportunity to allow our deepest longings, our needs and troubles to surface and be given their rightful place. Only then, with all the scaffolding shaken, can I admit how much I need to be rescued. Only then (to change the metaphor), when the walls and ramparts have been demolished and I have given up my plans for human perfection, will anything be possible. André Louf says that it is when we can say 'All this is beyond me!' that, in the words of Abba Moses, 'God comes to the rescue with his miracle'.[4]

It is when I am fully aware of my plight that I can hope to change, and to regain what was lost in the garden of Eden.

Thus humility and hope together make the start of the return journey. For Bernard emphasises the dignity of human nature, the human being as a 'lofty creature in its capacity for greatness'. As Merton says, it is clear that Bernard vindicates the fundamental goodness of human nature 'in terms as strong as have ever been used by any philosopher or theologian'.[5]

So we are split, and one half is this greatness: our likeness to and our capacity for union with God. Merton, in commenting in *The Spirit of Simplicity*, under the section 'Humility is Truth', is so emphatic about this that he puts it into capital letters!

> St Bernard would have us realise that there is another ignorance which is just as dangerous as the ignorance of our nothingness. It is paradoxically the ignorance of OUR OWN GREATNESS . . . If we do not know our own greatness we will never be able to have sufficient trust in God. If we do not realise that our greatness is from Him, and we are nothing of ourselves, then we will not even bother to trust in God, will rely entirely on ourselves.[6]

We must guard carefully against this ignorance which would make us esteem ourselves as less than God has made us, Bernard warns us, nor must we neglect 'our peculiar glory'. But equally we must steer clear of the opposing error, which would lead us to attribute to ourselves more than in fact we have, which we do when we regard God's gifts as though they were our own, when we forget from whom our greatness comes. In the first case we lose our own glory, in the second we glorify ourselves on account of that which is not ours.

A gentle and humble love? The connection between love and humility is not a usual one for us today when we expect the expression of love to be outgoing, active. Yet André Louf reminds us how important it is to remember what the monastic tradition says here. 'It is only in weakness that real love can make its contact.' This is a love that means being open to the other, receptive, listening and gentle, allowing the other to impinge, accepting the poverty of recognising that we need the other. 'Genuine love and friendship is impossible without humility; otherwise it is a stifling love.'[7] But there is also a further connection, which the Cistercian tradition helps us to explore, and that is between humility, love and knowledge. Humility is knowing our true position, the truth of who we are. Blinded by deceit, duplicity, illusion, we find that humility leads to self-knowledge.

Since Cistercian theology is so intimately personal and experiential Cistercian writing is inevitably bound to take a psychological direction. There was an added urgency to find answers to age-old questions. They wanted to know the nature of the soul, the presence and action of God in the soul, as they also needed to know the nature of the God who had created that soul in his image and likeness; and above all, since God created the human person for union with himself by charity, they also needed to know the nature of the action and degrees of charity. So if we are to try to grasp something of their approach to the mystery of love, the love of God, of others and of our own selves, we have to begin with their understanding of the human person. Therefore, though it might at first sight seem paradoxical, an essential Cistercian concern was the re-establishment of the integrity of human nature. 'The approach of the Cistercian fathers is a deliberate restoration and renewal of the human person', in the words of a present-day abbot.[8]

The first step in the Cistercian return to God, this God who is love, is for the monk to know himself. The root idea is announced by Bernard by an appeal to the Song of Songs 1:7: to know whence we came, where we stand, where we go is to know what we were, what we are, and what we are to be – to know ourselves. This is the true science and one that the Cistercian needs if he wants to walk in the way of love. From the outset of his teaching, therefore, Bernard turns aside from speculative philosophy to go more deeply into this interior study – which is of course a long tradition formed amongst the Greeks and continued by the Church Fathers, above all by Augustine. For how can we strip away these layers which have covered the divine likeness and overlaid our true greatness until we recognise them, until we know ourselves for what we have become?

So we are faced with this task: the need to know our own selves as we set out to make our way back to God. We have to understand how our human nature works, and what is natural to a human being made in the image and likeness of that triune God. This is perhaps the most significant and inescapable of human undertakings. But it is also one that is likely to be both hard and long, probably a lifetime's work, for it means uncovering layer after layer of our innermost selves. If we have to face the truth about ourselves we have to recognise the extent of our own duplicity, and to overcome the temptation to make excuses for ourselves. If, however, we are to seek the God of love who is seeking us it is the one task that we must take seriously, and this is where I have found myself so greatly helped by the twelfth-century Cistercians, for whom the question held such a peculiar fascination.

Bernard's treatment of the fall can be summed up: man lost his likeness to his creator and exemplar but retained the image, ingrained in and inseparable from the very essence of his soul. His teaching on this theme of image and likeness is above all a spiritual anthropology of return to God. There is human tragedy: the constant self-contradiction generated in us by the confrontation between the essential image of God and the lost likeness, or the disfigurement by sin. But there is this promise, the possibility of regaining the wholeness of the image and likeness in which we were originally created. In the first chapter of Genesis we are told that God made each one of us in his own image and likeness. But through sin, through the fall, we lost that likeness. The sin was the sin of pride, to think that human beings could become gods by natural right, not by grace. This image was not destroyed; but remains, hidden in the soul, however disfigured. Merton used the phrase a 'double' garment, which suggests living a lie of hypocrisy, or with an overlying layer of duplicity, which is not our real self and of which therefore we must rid ourselves.

Although we have retained the image we are not of course the Image itself, for only Christ is that; we are a copy of the Image. Here is the basis of the possibility of recovery. We are *capax Dei*, capable of God, capable of union with him. The image in us is indestructible. At one point Bernard used the marvellous phrase, calling the image 'this manifest sign of the divine generosity'. Here is a perpetual reminder from the Word that we have strayed but can return. So if we now live with disequilibrium we also live with the possibility, through conversion, of making a return.

This divine image which we have retained consists of three things: our freedom, that is to say our inborn freedom of will, which is where we are most like God; our natural simplicity, and our natural immortality. The greatness of the human being consists not merely in our own simplicity but in our ability to rise to participation in the infinitely perfect simplicity of the Word.

Sometimes we are given a more trinitarian emphasis, and reminded that we were created in the image of God, Father, Son and Spirit. 'Man was fashioned in the image of the Trinity,' wrote Aelred, 'his memory held fast to God without forgetfulness, his understanding recognised him without error, and his love embraced him without the self-centred desire for anything' – and he concluded with that wonderful declaration, 'and so man was happy'. William of St Thierry tells us from the moment of creation God the Holy Trinity takes possession of the soul, so that even after the fall there is still within us this 'natural structure' which drags, pulls us towards the Trinity. According to the intention of God there are in us three elements, memory, reason and will, which form the higher part of the soul and are the image of the holy Trinity in us. We should be occupied in the constant remembrance, knowledge and love of God. In this way we shall be sharing in the life of the Trinity. In *On the Song*, written in 1135, he says, 'Be totally present to yourself, and make total use of yourself, so that you can discern what you are and what you can do in him whose image you are.'

It is this innate, indestructible freedom that is to be, as it were, the point of contact, of union, of the soul with God. What has happened is that we have lost this freedom! Bernard says that when he speaks of our dignity or worthiness he means our free will, for it is this which renders us superior to all other living creatures. But this freedom has become twisted and perverted, in Merton's words, 'bending it back upon itself so that God's grace cannot get into it, cannot establish contact with it'.[9] So although this image still endures it is ruined – or in the word which Gilson uses, warped, while the Latin word *curvatura* gives me a visual sense of disfigurement or deformity. I am being presented with the contrast between this twisted self and my uprightness, *rectitudo*, and the hope is that I shall point upwards instead of being bent down towards the ground.

Bernard uses other ways of describing this, saying that we have become exiles, or that we are living with the inversion of right order. But however it is expressed it is always this contrast between two forces at war within me, deformity and conformity. My natural dignity and freedom are obscured by my abuse of free choice, and my self-centredness. My love gets directed away from God and turns towards what is inferior, and as a result I cannot take on the form of the divine likeness for which I was intended by God.

But Bernard is optimistic – he speaks of us being 'recalled to hope'. I see my deformity as an evil and I am drawn to the good which I see in myself underlying it all. In the words of Bernard, with parenthetical explanations added by Merton, the soul is

> drawn toward desperation by so great an evil
> (that is, its deformity)
> but recalled to hope by such goodness
> (the image of God perceived beneath the deformity).
> Hence it is that the more it is displeased by the evil
> it sees within itself,

the more ardently is it drawn to the good,
which it likewise spies in itself.[10]

The re-establishment of the integrity of human nature is
therefore precisely the central problem which Cistercian mysticism tackles. We are given the responsibility of making the
journey of restoration of what has been lost. The indispensable
condition for divine union is the recovery of what is natural to
us, our inborn freedom, our spontaneity, our *rectitudo*. The
task that each of us has to undertake is that of restoration,
renewal. It is of course one that the monastic way knows well,
for it is nothing less than the way of monastic conversion, the
return of the prodigal to the loving father. Everything with
the Cistercians, as Merton saw, 'leads them without delay
to the God they sought so ardently – the God of love'.

So I begin to see the way in which knowledge and humility
and love are all interconnected. God is love. Love, which is
given to us by God, makes it possible to know him – love is the
necessary condition of any knowledge of God. If we had nothing
in ourselves of what God is we would be incapable of knowing
him. *Amor ipse intellectus est*. This dictum is used in patristic
and Cistercian theology to express that loving a person,
especially God, is also a way of knowing that person, and
consequently being like that person by participation in what
that person is.[11]

But the further step is the distinction, so important with
Bernard, between the Charity which is God, and the charity
which is the gift of God in us, which is a gift of the Holy Spirit,
and which alone puts us in a position to know God. 'You are
the source of Love.' The primary source of love is God's love
for us. When there is so much talk of love and loving, so much
expectation heaped upon human loving which naturally it fails
to sustain, it is so refreshing to turn to Cistercian writings
and find help from men soaked in the word of God and in
prayer and filled with a humble self-knowledge.

John of Forde has his own 'hymn to love' which comes near
the end of his life. He sweeps us up into his great song of

praise of a God who in the beginning created the world out of his power and his love, and then sent his son into that world. For thirty years Jesus kept silence and then he opened his mouth: 'So the Wisdom of God has come, preaching to the world the love of God. And Jesus cries out: "God so loved the world as to give his Only-begotten Son".' God's love for us flows out from his very Being. Here is incontrovertible evidence which we cannot hesitate to accept – that God loved the world so much that he sent his Son into the world. And then John adds this mysteriously beautiful sentence: 'He gave this evidence in the waters, he gave it also in the floods'. Hilary Costello of Mount St Bernard comments that it is clear that he is here referring to the waters of suffering and death through which Jesus passed and came home safely to the harbour of his resurrection and eternal life. As with all images it speaks to each of us in its own terms – the waves that threaten to overwhelm us, the waters that come into our soul.

At one point in this sermon John of Forde speaks of the need for each of us to listen. 'Listen, O Church of God. To you the words are spoken, and to you alone have been given ears that can hear.'

> Listen!
> Consider the great Majesty
> of him who has loved you,
> how he has loved you from all eternity,
> how undeserved this love has been,
> how great it is.

John gives us the distinction between the three forms of love: the love with which God loves; the love by which he is loved; and the love by which we love our neighbour in God. This last is a fire, a fire that cannot be extinguished, which comes from God's own love. The primary source of this inextinguishable love is God's love of us – this is the bottom line, to which we return time and time again.[12]

Bernard also looks at the different sorts of love, and presents us with the different stages of loving. He distinguishes four degrees of love. The first is when we love ourselves for our selves. This is likely to bring us to a sense of our own need, our misery, and as a result to seeing that we need God. 'Recurrent troubles throw us back on God and each occasion proves how kind he is.' But by dint of turning to God out of need, this experience of his sweetness, in turn, provides an urge to the pure love of God since we soon begin to feel that to live with God is sweet. Thus we begin to love him for himself, though still torn between a pure love and a self-interested love. This is the stage in which we remain for the longest time, nor indeed do we ever emerge from it wholly in this life. For the fourth stage is the beatific vision which awaits us in heaven which is when we love ourselves only for God's sake. When he comes to write about this, in *De Diligendo Deo*, 'On the Love of God', Bernard can only call it God's 'own high hill', a mountain, strong, fertile and rich.

Towards the end of this treatise Bernard gives us a summary of what has gone before:

> The first point to consider is,
> that God deserves exceeding love from us,
> a love that has no measure.
> This is the first thing you must understand.
> The reason is, as I have said before,
> that he was first to love;
> He, who is so great, loves us so much . . .
> He, the unmeasured and eternal God,
> he who is love beyond all human ken,
> whose greatness knows no bounds,
> whose wisdom has no end, loves.
> Shall we, then, set a limit to our love for him?
> I will love thee, O Lord my strength,
> my stony rock and my defence,
> my saviour,
> my one desire and love.
> My God, my helper,
> I will love thee with all the power thou hast given me;

not worthily, for that can never be,
but to the full of my capacity . . .
I will love thee more and more,
as thou seest fit to give the further power;
yet never, never, as thou should'st be loved.

In the end Bernard brings us to the image of marriage. He gives us the language of the bedchamber, the kiss, the lover and the beloved. He writes about love as desire. The Song of Songs was for him, as for so many others in the Middle Ages, the source above all for the traditional mystical interpretation of the relationship between the lover and the beloved, between the soul and God. It was the book most read and most commented on in medieval monasteries. Bernard's commentary is undoubtedly his greatest and most important single work, 'the masterpiece of medieval monastic literature' in the words of Jean Leclercq. His writing is intense, artistic, rhythmical, in a highly sophisticated Latin to which translation cannot do justice. Perhaps it was originally delivered in chapter? Jean Leclercq asks this, saying that Bernard needed to express himself: 'To find an outlet for his inner fervour, he has to communicate his love, and in expressing it he feels it still more intensely.' For when we read it, as those first monks of Clairvaux heard it, it speaks to us because he is sharing with us what he had himself lived.[13]

Mystical marriage, or transforming union, may be terms which ring strangely for many of us, but they remain the end for which we were created in the image of God. Bernard told us that the divine image was implanted in our natures by God as an ineradicable reminder of our destiny to perfect union with him. He now shows us that each one of us, no matter how laden with sin,

overwrought by business, constricted by fear . . . has within itself the ability of turning back, not only to where it can breathe in the hope of pardon, in the hope of mercy, but even to where it can aspire to the nuptials of the Word, where it, a base creature, shall not be afraid to enter into

fellowship with God, nor be hesitant to bear, with the king
of angels, the yoke of love.

Merton calls this a magnificent passage which sums up
Bernard's providential message to his world and to our own,
as much needed today as it was in the twelfth century when
it was first heard and helped to bring in to Clairvaux those
'miraculous catches' of men.[14]

His eighty-third sermon on the Song of Songs, written at
the end of his life, treats the question of marriage at great
depth.

> Rightly does the bride renounce all other affections
> in order to give herself entirely to loving.
> It is in returning love that she responds to love
> and even if she totally poured herself forth in love,
> this would be little in comparison
> with that ever-flowing current which is its source.
> For there is no comparison in the volume of flow
> of lover and Love,
> of soul and Word,
> of bride and Bridegroom,
> of Creator and creature,
> no more than there is a comparison
> between one who is thirsty and the running spring.[15]

This marriage is something to which we may all aspire.
Sermon 83 opens with this magnificent declaration. So what
do we do? All we need to do is to return to the Word by charity,
and this work will be performed in our souls by the Word
himself. As soon as I am in a position to receive God's love
into my soul there is no doubt at all that he will not delay in
completing the good work that he started. As God looks on
what is happening and sees the likeness of his Son
reappearing, or as Merton puts it, 'as the simplicity of the
concealed image begins to be freed from the dark crust of sin',
he instantly pours more love into the soul, to encourage, and

to lead on to the perfect union of wills with God, by love, which is what Bernard means by mystical marriage.

The fullness of life which is the ultimate goal of the Rule and which the Cistercian founding fathers set out to attain is the perfection of love in the experience of God. So we can see this 'mystical element' of the Cistercian way as nothing more than the full flowering of seeds sown by Benedict. Benedict wanted his monks to 'come to that perfect love of God which casts out fear'. In the final words of the Rule he asked 'Are you hastening towards your heavenly home?' And then, he adds, 'You can set out for the loftier summits . . .' For Bernard the twelve-step ladder of chapter 7 leads directly to perfect love, to the delights and joys of contemplation. It takes us on to the chamber of the king where the soul 'rests secretly in the king's embrace. While in this chamber the soul sees things that the human eye cannot see and hears mysteries that no tongue can repeat . . .' The commentary on the Song of Songs is for the Cistercians the equivalent of a treatise on the love of God, for, as an anonymous monk from the abbey of Pontigny said, it is a poem of the pursuit which is the goal, the whole programme, of the monastic life. It is the dialogue between two persons seeking one another, calling to one another, growing nearer to one another. It is a contemplative text which with its ardent language is more attuned than any other book of the Bible to loving contemplation.[16]

'For the love of Christ' sums up quite simply the end of the Cistercian life. They explored it with a loving intensity but it would have no resonance with us today if it did not come from the heart, from lives in which the experience of knowing and loving Christ was a reality. Walter Daniel describes Aelred being on his deathbed for three days, for his spirit remained strong even though his body was frail.

> Over and again we heard him say 'Hasten, hasten', often gracing the words with the name of Christ, and in English too, for the word having only one syllable in that language it comes easier to the lips and is somewhat sweeter

sounding to the ear. So he would say, to use his own words, 'Hasten, for Crist luve': that is, 'for the love of Christ, hasten.'[17]

8. THE SHARING OF LOVE

But for our love of others to be wholly right,
God must be at its root.
No one can love his neighbour perfectly,
unless it is in God he holds him dear.
And nobody can love his fellow-men in God
who loves not God himself.
We must begin by loving God;
and then we shall be able, in him, to love our neighbour
  too.[1]

Bernard makes the connection: we have the two commandments of charity, love of God and love of neighbour. Spiritual
experience may be for Bernard a pathway to the discovery of
the true self in God, but it is no less a reaching out to others.
Even the greatest contemplative gifts, even the deepest personal intimacy with God, find their context within, and are to
some sense, ordered to life in community, to the 'pure love of
brothers' of the Rule.

A sense of community still came naturally to a world which
was discovering the self but had not yet discovered the individual; from birth everyone knew that they belonged in the
family, the village or town, the immediate locality and the
wider region, the workers' gild, the students' corps, the monastic community and, not least, the greater community of the
Church, the whole Body of Christ.

When Bernard spoke of 'a true and deep and universal and
supernatural love for other men' this was nothing abstract: it
came out of his own experience. From the Cistercians we learn

about corporate love, for they not only worked hard at living it but they explored it in words. They did so with the zeal that came from their commitment to the way of Benedict as, above all, a sharing of love. Everything leads up to that panegyric of love in chapter 72, the penultimate chapter of the Rule, 'The good zeal of monks'. There Benedict uses the word fervent love, *fervens*, white hot, burning. The man known for his balance and moderation becomes a passionate man, looking for 'hearts overflowing with the inexpressible delight of love'. In his portrait of the abbot, the father of the community, the exemplar of Christ to the brothers, he shows us love at work, strong and firm, honest in discernment, and also patient, gentle, compassionate.

William of St Thierry, in his *Vita Prima*, his biography of Bernard, gives us a portrait of Bernard the abbot, father figure to his monks, but his words would be no less true of William himself.

> His brethren became for him a great joy, and with them he shared his delight in the fruitful results of his entry into the monastic life . . . one could follow his perfect example of how life should be led in complete and loving conformity with the Rule as he organised his monastery and took part in all its many activities. He was indeed building a dwelling place for God on earth . . . He learned to consider the weak and feeble by sympathising in their weaknesses . . . for others he was full of tenderness and care . . .[2]

Aelred was for twenty years the abbot of Rievaulx, and here we can see this 'pure love of brothers', as he acted as father, pastor, physician, judge, brother to all the differing types of men who crowded into his monastery. His biographer Walter Daniel tells us that monks in want of brotherly understanding and compassion came flocking to Rievaulx from the farthest ends of the earth and found peace there. In a famous passage he says: 'This man turned Rievaulx into a veritable stronghold for the comfort and support of the weak, the fostering of the strong and sound, an abode of peace and piety where God and neighbour might be loved in fullest measure.'

Aelred himself said that he wanted Rievaulx to be a place of love strong and open enough to admit everyone, however weak and imperfect, just as Noah's ark must save all kinds of creatures, though he added that we should distinguish the place where we put them, like rooms in the ark, according to the different kinds of love we owe them.[3] Benedict had made the exercise of discretion, or discernment, an essential part of the role of abbot, recognising that everyone has his gift from God (*Rule*, 40.1) and there are both natural differences and also differences in grace. Writing about this life at Rievaulx, Merton commented that through his art of appropriate loving Aelred would be brought

> more and more deeply into the abyss of God's love and God's mercy, for he was able to contemplate, in the growth and transformation of the souls entrusted to him, something of God that he could never have experienced in any other way, even in the depths of the most perfect contemplative union with him.[4]

In his sermon *de Diversis* Bernard said:

> It is a glorious thing for men to dwell together in one house with one mind. How good and how pleasant to see brothers living in unity! You can see one lamenting his sins, another praising God; this one ministering to all, another teaching and instructing; this one praying, that one reading. One confesses his sins, another does penance for his. One shines for his charity, another for his humility. One can be seen to be humble in prosperity, another patient in adversity; this one is engaged in work, another rests in contemplation. Thus we can say: Truly this is the camp of God . . . [Genesis 32:2].[5]

This amazingly mixed and diverse group of men complemented and completed one another. Their goal was to live as 'one heart and one mind': mutual participation, the sharing of things in common, service, companionship. Charity, love with a Christ-dimension, becomes a unitive force, forming one heart and one life, forging the many into one.

But there is this paradoxical situation: if the goal of community life is that men have come together to seek the contemplative presence of God in quietness of soul, in attentiveness to the Word and above all in that true silence which is interior silence, what does this sharing mean? Guerric gives us his answer in this passage:

> By the wonderful favour of God's loving care, in this solitude of ours we have the peace of solitude and yet we do not lack the consolation and comfort of holy companionship. It is possible for each of us to sit alone and be silent, because we have no one to disturb us with interruptions, and yet it cannot be said of us: 'Woe to him who is alone, since he has nobody to console him or if he should fall has none to lift him up'. We are surrounded by companions, yet we are not in a crowd.[6]

Here is a climate for contemplative prayer, produced by a shared desire to become channels of God's words to each other: 'I reckon as God's my own word, my brethren, whatever the Holy Spirit in his mercy sees fit to speak within you – every single word which avails to build up faith, stirring up love.' Guerric told his monks that they must start to use words 'that are, as it were, God's own, so that no bad word, even in private conversation, should cross one's lips'. This constant, loving, fraternal ministry of the Word is one of the things that the monk seeks in community, so that the support of his brothers deepens the contemplative life. Guerric has no illusions: 'We live on two levels, partly according to the flesh, partly according to the spirit.' It will be easier for some than for others, but the obligation is the same for everyone. 'For it is the power and nature of true love that even when it does not feel affection it nevertheless contrives to make itself loved in return.' In this way, Guerric says, 'You show that you really are a brother among brothers in all your dealings.'

The love of God and the love of neighbour belong together. Both flow from the fact that from the beginning God himself has practised these two commandments. The Father loved his only Son, and the Son loved the Father. The Father loved the Son who was God – and therefore practised the love of God; and in loving him he loved his neighbour who was his Son. John of Forde's teaching was based on this very simple, but splendid and original theological understanding.[7] So when we ask the question: how are we then to love, the answer is that Christ came to show us how to love. This is the importance of the incarnation. If we imitate Christ we imitate his compassion and his obedient love. Through the incarnation and through his death on the cross we are given the example of an out-pouring of love. *Deus caritas est*: God is love. This is the Gospel of St John once again, the keystone of this theology of love.

What then was involved in *communio*? To share, to have all things in common, like the community in Jerusalem described in the first seven chapters of Acts, who were such an important example to them, as we have seen already. To be open to the good of all was also a sign of being open to God: having nothing of one's own is to need others, and more than that, to need God. Here is the 'one heart and soul' which was the special inspiration for the Cistercians. John of Forde said of them:

> There was certainly a unity of purpose in this city (the new Jerusalem, community of the early disciples). Here all shared the one utterance and the same mind towards God and each other. All together because of their united hearts; all in one place, because of their patience. There was union in the deepest charity and in the fellowship of the spirit, there was patience in the long, submissive waiting for the Holy Spirit. Anything that might be a stumbling block to charity, had already been banished far from that city . . .[8]

Aelred spoke in terms of a mutual harmony, a 'complete agreement in all things divine and human':

Each one of you before coming here, had a single soul that was wholly yours. You have been converted to God, and behold, the Holy Spirit, the fire from heaven that Our Lord has sent upon the earth and would see kindled, has reached your hearts, has reached your souls, and out of all your hearts and souls has made one heart and one soul.

Gilbert of Hoyland preached on the same theme in these words:

And there is no dwelling together in unity unless it be in love – love which brings those with a common way of life under the same roof. What is it to have a common way of life but to be conformed by the bond of love?[9]

There is a double movement within love – the love of sharing and the sharing of love, two movements, which cannot be separated one from the other. If this is missing, Baldwin of Forde tells us, then love is not happy, for it seeks its joy and its happiness not only in the sharing of goods but also in the sharing of its own self:

Love, by a certain instinctive movement,
longs to pour itself forth
and transfer the good it possesses
to someone it loves with all its love;
it longs to have it in common,
to take the other as a companion
and to share its possessions with him.
In the view of charity,
everything good shines with a more beautiful light –
when – so far as it is proper –
it is held in common with another.[10]

I particularly like that phrase 'to take the other as a companion', for it leads us into what I have found to be one of the most significant areas of the Cistercian understanding of love, and that is the role of friendship. God's love for us makes possible an infinite variety of human loves, of which friendship is one of the most blessed. Apart from Cassian this a word which occurs only rarely in the ancient monastic writers. But with the Cistercians it comes to the fore in a most vigorous way. Friendship was for them part of the economy of human salvation. If on the level of our relationship with God they speak of desire, when it comes to our relationship with others they can speak of *intimacy*. Thus they reclaim for us a word which has come to have narrowly sexual connotations and so allow us to celebrate the fullness of friendship.

At a convention in America which I recently attended the gospel reading at the eucharist was John 15:12–15, and afterwards, as we all sat in small groups for a biblical reflection, different in age, colour, race and background, the force of those words 'I have called you friends' came home to me. It was the bishop amongst us who commented on how God rearranges relationships, how revolutionary this is, ending any hierarchical emphasis with this, a radically new way. Christ, in calling us friends, has chosen us; he is looking for friends. This is making a momentous statement, and one which I see being overlooked when it has become so common today to talk about the model of the family, often equating church and family, and choosing to ignore the fact that rather over half the population are not members of a conventional family – and not necessarily from choice.

Aelred believed so much in the theological and spiritual reality of friendship that he even dared to paraphrase the familiar saying of John as: 'God is friendship and he who lives in friendship lives in God and God lives in him.' When he asked 'Was it not a foretaste of blessedness thus to love and to be loved?' he must surely have been thinking of his own experience of warm and intimate friendship. The friendship of the cloister brought men together in the common pursuit of the one friend whom they all shared, Christ himself. Aelred says that it is as a friend, a brother, that Christ presents himself in his humanity, in order to help us to love ourselves and our neighbours. He knew how a friend becomes the sacrament which reveals the love of Christ. He describes at length the marvellous process of grace whereby friendship between brothers leads into friendship with Christ, makes it grow, and deepens it. This friendship, like all other friendships, as André Louf comments, calls for 'reserve, silence, intimacy, interiority'.[11] There can be no spiritual friendship between two people without Christ as a third on whom each is centred. This in essence is the whole of Aelred's message. All aspects of friendship have their beginning, their continuance and their end in Christ.

His treatise *On Spiritual Friendship* is his most personal work, written towards the end of his life. It is in the form of a dialogue, as though a conversation is taking place between the abbot and three of the monks. This was a popular form of literary genre in the Middle Ages and it makes for entertaining reading. For example, at one point, Aelred is teasing Walter:

> Come now, brother, and explain why it was that, while I was providing earthly food for worldly minded men you were sitting alone and apart, now swivelling your eyes this way and that, now rubbing your forehead with your hand, now running your fingers through your hair, and looking by turns cross, querulous and recalcitrant.

We are included in the circle, given a sense of being present, feeling anxious that the bursar might come knocking on the door, or that the sun is sinking too fast and time is running out. It is almost as though we are eavesdropping upon the intimate sharing of this exploration of spiritual friendship. It is a subject that Aelred tells us has been of importance to him since his school days. He had first read Cicero's *De Amicitia* forty years before, and it still gave him much that he could use, though it was his later experience of monastic life which was even more significant. There are various levels on which he could draw: his own monastic family of Rievaulx (not least in the relationship of choir-monks and lay brothers); the wider perspective of the Cistercian Order and the way in which it recognised the importance of unity and diversity; the model of the house of Bethany, the two sisters who are friends, and their brother Lazarus, three different types of people who are living together harmoniously under one roof.

Aelred is wise, and realistic. He is concerned with the steps, the boundaries and the difficulties of friendship – there is no idea here that friendship just happens automatically. He writes vividly of how friendship can be built on childish whim, how it can blow hot and cold, how it can become like tentacles stretching out. He knows only too well how friendship can turn sour, how it can turn into physical desire, how it can lead to misunderstandings, hatred and jealousy, and indeed that it may have to be slowly dismantled, gently dissolved, and that there might have to be a period of disengagement. Former friends still have an obligation to show each other special love and loyalty; the bond must never cease, but there is also the right to maintain a distance in order to protect oneself.

But friendship represents a deep human longing, and need. 'Friendship is a twinning of minds and spirits where two become as one. Your friend is a second self from whom you withhold nothing, hide nothing, fear nothing.' 'The man without a friend is the man utterly alone. But what happiness, security and joy to have another self to talk to! . . . someone to whom you dare entrust all the secrets of your heart and in whose advice you can have confidence.' All the more urgent therefore that it should be built on a firm foundation, something which will anchor it and give it a firm footing. And that of course can only be the love of God.

> The fountainhead of friendship is love,
> for love can exist without friendship,
> but friendship without love, never.

And then Aelred gives us this great panegyric:

> The perfecting and extending of true friendship
> is the great and wondrous happiness
> that we look for in the life to come.
> God himself is at work

pouring out between himself and the creature he has
    raised up
between the various hierarchies of his creation,
and between each and every one of his elect
such reciprocal friendship and charity
that each loves the other as himself.
Each, in consequence, rejoices in his neighbour's
    happiness as his own,
so that the bliss of each is shared by all,
and the sum total of that bliss is everyone's.
This is the true and everlasting friendship,
which has its beginnings here,
and its consummation hereafter.
And if such reciprocity is hard to come by in this world
(since it is laid up for us beyond!)
should not our happiness grow according as we find it?[12]

There is also this wonderful passage about the community
of Rievaulx, the very living out of what *The Charter of Charity*
had set as its ideal:

The day before yesterday,
walking round the cloisters,
where the brethren were sitting,
as it were a very garland of love,
I was gazing on them,
as one might admire in paradise
the leaves and flowers and fruit of every individual tree,
and found none there whom I did not love,
and by whom I did not believe myself loved.
I was filled with a joy
that soared above all the pleasures of this world.
I felt my spirit pass out into all
and their affection flow back into me,
until I found myself saying with the Psalmist:
'Behold how good and how pleasant it is when brethren
    dwell together in unity.'[13]

9. PORTRAIT GALLERY

AELRED OF RIEVAULX

Aelred was born in 1110 in Northumbria, where both his father and his grandfather had been married priests at Hexham. He himself had a deep devotion to Cuthbert, which probably dated from his school days in Durham. He spent much of his early life in the entourage of King David I of Scotland, and at the age of twenty-two was made the King's steward. He was clearly marked out for a successful career when a chance remark on a journey on the King's business sent him off to visit the Abbey of Rievaulx, founded from Clairvaux in 1132.

He had eight years as a choir monk, a time for prayer and study which he often recalled with nostalgia. But in 1142, still only thirty-two, and quite young in the order, he was sent on an important mission to Rome where he met Bernard. When he returned he was appointed master of novices, a position of great responsibility in the early days of a monastery, when the whole tone of the place could so easily be altered by the influx of the new monks coming in. Aelred gave them conferences which were noted on wax tablets, or outlined on spare scraps of parchment from the scriptorium. But then there came a letter from Bernard himself, who had been impressed by his grasp and understanding. He ordered him to digest his notes into a treatise to be called *The Mirror of Charity*, and personally outlined the form it was to take.

In the following year Aelred was elected abbot of the community which had grown in the first ten years of its life to 300 monks and lay brothers, and was now almost to double again during his abbacy. Undoubtedly it was his personality which drew men flocking to Rievaulx 'from foreign countries and the farther ends of the earth' as Walter Daniel tells us, 'and finding the gates wide open, passed freely through them giving thanks to the Lord'.

Aelred wrote both spiritual and historical works (an interest generated during those years at court) and left in addition great numbers of sermons. Charles Cummings calls him one of the most approachable of twelfth-century Cistercians, and we can appreciate this, since we have in Walter Daniel's *Life* of him an account from someone who was under him at Rievaulx for seventeen years and knew him well. He touches on many things which are concerns today, above all his understanding of friendship.

He died in 1167, and Walter Daniel writes of waiting at the bedside until he 'was laid, as is the monastic custom, on a haircloth strewn with ashes, and there, amid the great gathering of sons . . . he died in the fourth watch of the night'.

BERNARD OF CLAIRVAUX

Bernard was born near Dijon, probably around 1090, and in his early twenties entered Cîteaux together with most of his brothers, and a number of friends and relations. Within three years he had become the first abbot of a new foundation, Clairvaux. Here his personal magnetism and his spiritual fervour were so far-reaching and irresistible that men came from the ends of Europe making the community, in the words of Pauline Matarasso, 'the brightest star in the monastic galaxy'. In 1130 Bernard found himself drawn away from Clairvaux into what was to become from now on an inescapable element in his life: the politics of Church and state. He continued to protest that he longed for solitude and quiet but he found himself increasingly embroiled in affairs outside the cloister, some of which, like the preaching of the Second Crusade, do not claim much sympathy from us today.

A complex, talented, combative, loving man, a reformer in

some things and a conservative in others, he is larger than life – though one thread holds it all together, and that is his zeal for the Church which was simply an extension of the love of God which directed and informed his whole being. Michael Casey summed up this fellow-Cistercian whom he has come to know as fully as anyone today: Bernard was a prophet, a man who found in the Word of God the energy to open doors for his contemporaries and communicate to them something of his zest for living and his enthusiasm for the way of Christ. This was his passion, his life, and no other image makes any sense.

He was a brilliant communicator, with a mastery of both the spoken and the written word. He had the gift of the prophet to understand those whom he addressed. He was totally a man of his time; his special genius was to translate the message of the gospel into terms acceptable to his day. People both listened to him and read his texts, which were copied and circulated widely. The finest flowering of his thought is undoubtedly to be found in the series of sermons on the Song of Songs but there is much else besides: treatises and conferences, theological tracts and biography, hymns and letters. He could express himself in any of these forms, but always it is the voice of the monk, a rich monastic doctrine and spirituality, that he brings to us today as he did to those who first encountered him in the twelfth century.

He died at Clairvaux in 1153.

GILBERT OF HOYLAND

Gilbert takes his name from the Fenland which borders on the Wash, though it is uncertain if he was born locally or came from Europe. All we know is that he was elected Abbot of Swineshead in 1150 and that he ruled over the community for the next twenty years. Like many others he found the burden of office hard and longed for more time for prayer and for writing. When Bernard died in 1153 leaving the commentary on the Song of Songs unfinished, Gilbert was asked by the

General Chapter of the Order to complete it. The fifty sermons that he was able to add to it before his own death in 1172 enjoyed a wide circulation. In addition he left seven short treatises and four letters which give us a glimpse of a man of a rich and lively imagination and a profound spirituality.

GUERRIC OF IGNY

Guerric of Igny is counted as one of the original 'four evangelists of Cîteaux' even though he is not so well known. He was born in Tournai, probably in the 1080s, and was a cleric, possibly a canon. His desire for a stricter life took him to Clairvaux around 1125, lured by the reputation of Bernard who then watched over his novitiate. Bernard thought so highly of him that he helped him to be elected as the second Abbot of Igny, a house dependent on Clairvaux, and there he remained until his death on 19 August 1157.

He was in his fifties or sixties when he was elected. He was a good abbot, he loved his monks, was open and frank with them, and laid before them solid, practical doctrine. He himself said that his one desire in preaching was to give his monks Jesus Christ. On his deathbed he ordered the book in which he had collected his sermons to be burned, but prudently his monks had had copies made. As a result we have fifty-four liturgical sermons, based on texts drawn from the liturgy of the day, gentle and elegiac in style. He loved the Scriptures and he loved above all to draw out their hidden meanings. He writes with simplicity and tenderness and is altogether one of the most lovable of these early Cistercians.

ISAAC OF STELLA

Very little is known of his life except the hints that can be gleaned from his writing. He was born around 1100, of English birth, but was drawn to France by the reputation of its schools. We do not know if he was professed at Pontigny or at Stella near Poitiers, but he was undoubtedly the Abbot of Stella by

1147. He died between 1167 and 1169 and has left fifty-five sermons and two treatises in letter form. From these we see a man who longed for the wilderness, and he may even have left his monastery to seek a life of greater solitude and austerity, though we cannot be sure of this. He gives us a theology that is rooted in Scripture, and his writing is figurative, symbolic and a delight to the ear.

JOHN OF FORDE

Until he entered the monastery which bears his name nothing is known of John. He was probably born around 1150, which puts him into the category of those who never knew Bernard or any of the first Cistercian generation personally. He was a Devon man and studied in the schools attached to Exeter Cathedral. When he entered Forde it must have been an exciting place under its abbot Baldwin (to be elevated quite soon to Canterbury), a community with an active learned tradition. He was prior there in 1184, and after a short exodus when he was elected as Abbot of Bindon, he returned in 1191. He was abbot for twenty-five years, at first years of comparative calm but clouded in later life by the country's political squabbles, and when he died in 1214 the land was still under the interdict imposed by Innocent III in 1208. Mass could be celebrated once a week in the monasteries but it was denied to the ordinary people and John felt great sadness at this. He was buried in his abbey church, without pomp, as he had lived. His sermons composed during the last and more troubled years of his life show us his serenity of spirit. His letters sadly are missing but a considerable body of his work remains, not least the 120 sermons that he wrote completing the commentary on the Song of Songs begun by Bernard and continued by Gilbert of Hoyland. His writing is saturated in the Scriptures and his emphasis on contemplation and his enjoyment of imagery make him one of the most sympathetic of all Cistercian writers.

THOMAS MERTON

Thomas Merton was born in January 1915 in the small town of Prades at the foot of the French Pyrenees where his parents, both of them artists, had chosen to live and paint. His early years were divided between France, England and America. His mother Ruth was American and his father Owen came from New Zealand. His mother died of cancer in 1921 when he was six, and at first he lived with his father in France, and later went to school in England and subsequently spent one year at Cambridge. When he returned to New York he went to Columbia and there continued the pattern of his English university time: parties and politics and girlfriends and drinking and talking, all the time lost, desperately searching. But when on 10 December 1941 he entered the monastery of Gethsemani in Kentucky he knew that he had come home. From then on he lived the Cistercian life, but with an increasing longing for solitude that was finally recognised when he was allowed to move into a little hermitage in the woods near the abbey. He developed an interest in Eastern monasticism and in Buddhism and in 1968 was give permission to leave the monastery in order to go to a conference in Bangkok. Here on 10 December (twenty-seven years to the day since he entered Gethsemani) he was accidentally electrocuted.

His enormous popularity, undiminished decades after his death, is probably largely due to the fact that here is a man who was above all things a monk, yet who writes about the monastic life and monastic theology in a way that appealed to lay people. He read, studied and taught in Gethsemani as the novice master, but he also wrote. He wrote because he had to write: it was a part of his life. His autobiography *A Seven Storey Mountain* became an instant best-seller and it is still the means by which many people come to know him and to identify with him. He wrote journals of his monastic life such as *The Sign of Jonas* and *A Vow of Conversation*. He wrote learned theology and he wrote political pamphlets. He was involved in the 1960s in issues of peace and justice and race. His correspondence was vast and is still in the process of being edited, as are his journals. He was also a considerable poet and a gifted photographer. His writing is uneven, much of the earlier material rather pious and full of purple patches. He shows us much of the monastic life for he was at once totally a monk and just as totally a fully human person of the twentieth century.

WILLIAM OF ST THIERRY

A native of Liége, William came from the ranks of the lesser nobility. He may have studied under Anselm before becoming a Benedictine monk. He met Bernard in 1120, the year in which he was elected Abbot of St Thierry, near to Rheims. This was painful for he longed now only to live at Clairvaux and to continue the friendship which he had formed with Bernard – for he had fallen under his spell at their first meeting. Bernard, however, was adamant that he must not escape his responsibilities and so William remained at Thierry for the next fifteen years and struggled with his desire for a more contemplative life. Finally he joined a group of monks who were leaving the monastery of Igny to found a daughter house at Signy in the Ardennes, and that is where he lived until his death in 1148.

Even though he was a black monk (i.e., Benedictine) for most of his life he was a Cistercian in spirit from the time of his first visit to Clairvaux. He was the biographer of Bernard and reverenced him as his master – though in fact he was by no means his intellectual inferior. It is only in this century that he has been rescued from being under Bernard's shadow. Much of his writing that earlier had been neglected or attributed to Bernard is now recognised as by this markedly original thinker. Pauline Matarasso says that the two currents – intellectual/metaphysical and affective/mystical – which had hitherto flowed together in a common Christian tradition but were soon to divide, can be found in his writings still perfectly intermingled.

His earliest work, *On Contemplating God*, was written in 1165, and after that a huge amount of original work flowed from his pen. His writings showed a marked interest in that self-knowledge which the twelfth century saw as a prerequisite to the knowledge of God, and in him we find an interest in human psychology seen always as a key to spiritual understanding. Of his *Golden Epistle* it has been said it is, philosophically speaking, the most solid body of work to emanate from a Cistercian environment. His final and uncompleted work was a labour of love, a biography of his much-loved master and friend Bernard. At the end of the section on him in *Last of the Fathers*, Basil Pennington says that 'the wise, beautiful, simple but sublime teaching of this blessed abbot still attracts, encourages and leads countless people, both in the cloister and outside it, to the true fulfilment of man, a deep loving union with God in Christ'.

10. *LECTIO*[1]

He himself is my meditation;
he is my delight;
him for his own sake I seek above me;
from him himself I feed within me.
He is the field in which I labour;
he is the fruit for which I labour.
He is my cause;
he is my effect.
He is my beginning;
he is my end without end.
He is for eternity.

Ipse mihi meditatio,
Ipse mihi delectatio.
Ipsum propter ipsum super me quaero.
Ipso ab ipso inter me pasco.
Ipse mihi ager in quo laboro,
Ipse mihi fructus pro quo laboro,
Ipse mihi causa,
Ipse mihi effectus,
Ipse mihi principium,
pse mihi finis sine fine,
Ipse mihi in aeternum.

SEEKING GOD

It is enchanting enough to seek you,
O good Jesus,
but more enchanting to hold you.
The former is a devout task,
the latter perfect joy.

THE HEART AS A WELL OF JOY

You will make the well of your heart
deep and capacious
if you remove earthly cares,
if you prepare in your spirit
for spiritual joy,
if you open your mouth
to draw in the spirit
and if streams of living water
flow into your heart.

THE EXPANDING HEART

Come to expand our hearts
with the calm, smooth flow of your bounty, O Lord,
since I ran the way of your commands,
when you expanded my heart,
and since you stretch out the sky like a hide,
now smoothly stretch out the hide of my heart
grown old and shrivelled in an idle breast.
Unfold its wrinkles,
draw out its hiding places,
enlarge its vessels,
that without measure
I may yearn for you,
without measure contain you,
and that your holy capacity
may give me greater capacity.

AT HOME IN MYSELF

The house in which we live is ourselves,
provided we remain at home to ourselves
and are not drawn outside of ourselves by desire for
  error.
The door-posts are the body and the soul.
We put the blood of the lamb on each post,
when we imitate the sufferings of Christ
through affliction of body and soul.
The lintel is a devout intention,
and blood is put upon it when the intention of our
  thoughts
is directed to the imitation of the sufferings of Christ.
Those who are signed
are those who imitate Christ by suffering with him,
and who put the sign of life on their lives.

COMPASSION FOR ONESELF

When your household sits down to a meal,
if you are wise,
you will first sit down yourself,
and then you will be able to serve them
easily and happily.
In your charity to your neighbour,
remember that your nearest neighbour is yourself.

REST

> Even as the sun was bestowed upon the world by
>   God to give light
> it still ought to turn aside fairly frequently,
> to have a time for peace and quiet . . .
> it ought to know how to set
> and be at rest in the evening,
> when it enters the embrace of leisure.

THE POWER OF PRAYER

The bodily appearance of the Lord was changed as
   he prayed
and thereby he wished to bring home to your mind
the power of prayer,
because prayer
makes you different in your inmost being
and meditation
changes you into a new self
and renews you.
'With our unveiled faces reflecting like mirrors
the brightness of the Lord' says Paul,
'we are turned into the image which we reflect',
that is, we are transformed
into the very image we gaze upon.

THE HEALING SHADOW

After we had lain so long in the shadow of death,
God's Son came, pitying those who lay in darkness.
He made us lie down
under the shadow of another apple tree,
and by that shadow
as much as by its fruits
he raised us to life again.
He came that we may have life
and have it more abundantly.

SUFFERING

> If for your food
> you have been given gall,
> if in your thirst
> you have drunk vinegar,
> remember that Jesus suffered the like.

THE SOUTH WIND

Execute your command, Good Jesus;
dispatch the south wind from heaven
and conduct it into your garden,
into the soul of your bride.
By this gentle breeze dispel boredom,
dispel sadness from her feelings,
for each is a misery
and each resembles the north wind;
each fetters the mind, as it were,
and bars access
to the current of pure joy.

TURNING FROM SADNESS

Therefore, my advice to you, friends,
is to turn aside from troubled and anxious reflection
   on your own progress,
and escape to the easier paths of remembering the
   good things God has done.
In this way, instead of becoming upset by thinking
   about yourself,
you will find relief by turning your attention to
God . . .
Sorrow for sin is indeed a necessary thing,
but it should not prevail all the time.
On the contrary, it is necessary that happier
   recollections of God's generosity
should counterbalance it,
lest the heart should become hardened through too
   much sadness
and so perish through despair.

THE CROSS

Before the cross every knee is bowed;
before the cross every tongue confesses Christ.
This is the throne of grace;
this is the fount of mercy.
This is the place of forgiveness;
this is where breasts are beaten,
and crimes confessed and dismissed.
This is where supplications and prayers are poured
    forth,
where heartfelt groans and sighs are poured out ...
Hither you come, all you who labour and are heavy-
    laden,
and all who have fallen short
and are in need of the grace of God.
The mercy of God has been plainly placed before our
    eyes,
the grace of salvation has been revealed in the sight
    of all peoples.
Acknowledge the utility of the cross;
acknowledge its power and dignity!

THE NEWNESS OF LOVE

The dawn of a soul that loves God rises up,
I do not say every day,
but all day,
never tiring.
For if one truly loves,
then each hour seems like the dawn of fresh love.
It was of charity that it is written in Scripture,
'I shall put a new spirit within you',
and, 'A new commandment I give you'.
There is a sense in which what is perpetually new,
is perpetually at the beginning.
In fact, newness continually holds within itself its
   own beginning,
so as to seem always at the point of starting,
since it is wholly unaffected by decay or age.

THE INTERACTION OF LOVES

That a person may love himself,
the love of God is formed in him;
that one may love one's neighbour,
the capacity of one's heart is enlarged.
Then as this divine fire grows warmer
little by little
it wondrously absorbs the other loves into its
    fullness,
like so many sparks.
And so it leads all the soul's love with it
to that supreme and ineffable good
where neither self nor neighbour is loved for self or
    for neighbour
but only insofar as each fades away from self
and is borne totally into God.

Meanwhile, these three loves
are engendered by one another,
nourished by one another,
and fanned into flame by one another.
Then they are all brought to perfection together.

SERVICE TO OTHERS

May my thoughts and my speech,
leisure and labour,
my acts and reflections,
my prosperity and my adversity,
my life and my death,
my health and sickness, and whatsoever else is mine:
that I exist,
that I live,
that I feel,
that I understand:
let all be devoted to them
and all be spent for them,
for whom thou thyself did not disdain to spend
   thyself.

GOD AT ALL TIMES

He is the remedy for our wounds.
He is help in time of trouble.
He is the source of repair
for those who are falling back,
and he is the source of abundance
for those who advance.
Finally he is the means by which human beings
have or receive whatever is good and appropriate for
them.

CHRIST OUR COMPANION

When men grow weary of studying spiritual doctrine
and become lukewarm,
when their spiritual energies are drained away,
then they walk in sadness along the ways of the
    Lord.
They fulfil the tasks enjoined on them
with hearts that are tired and arid,
they grumble without ceasing.
If when we are subject to these moods,
the compassionate Lord draws near to us on the way,
and being from heaven begins to talk to us about
    heavenly truths,
sings our favourite airs from the songs of Zion,
speaks about the city of God and its peace,
and on the life that is eternal,
I assure this happy talk will drive away all tension
from the hearer's mind
    and weariness from his body.

THE INCOMPREHENSIBILITY OF GOD

The blessed soul has also a higher manner of loving
that gives it no little labour within,
namely when it is drawn into a love
beyond what is human,
beyond human sense and reason,
and beyond all the works of our heart.

It is drawn through eternal Love alone
into the eternity of Love,
and into the incomprehensibility
and vastness
and inaccessible sublimity
and deep abyss of the Godhead,
which is totally present in all things
and remains incomprehensible beyond all things,
which is immutable,
perfect Being,
all-powerful,
all-intelligent,
almightily operating.

LIGHT

Ah! brothers,
look where the candle burns in Simeon's hands;
that is the light to light your tapers from,
those lamps which the Lord would have you holding.
Go to him and you will be lit up;
not so much bearers of lamps
as lamps yourselves,
shining within and without,
lighting yourselves and your neighbours.
May this lamp be in heart and hand and mouth:
a lamp in your heart to light yourself;
a lamp in your hands and on your lips
to light your neighbours.
The light in your heart is loving faith;
the lamp in your hands is the example of good deeds;
the lamp on your lips, helpful and strengthening
    words.
    . . .
So that you may light all these lamps for yourselves,
    my brethren,
come to the source of light and be enlightened.
    . . .
When all your lamps are lighted, sons of light,
you will not walk in darkness,
nor will you need to fear the condemnation.
    . . .
as for you for whom so many lamps are shining,
you will see,
when your lamp of life is doused,
the light of life undying
rise like the blaze of noon in your evening sky.

And just when you thought your candle had burned
   down,
you will flame up again
and your darkness will be like noonday.
You will not need the glory of the sun to light you
   by day,
nor will the moonlight shine on you,
but the Lord will be your everlasting light:
for the Lamb is the lamp of the new Jerusalem,
to whom be all blessing and radiance of glory
for ever and ever. Amen.

SYMBOL OF LIGHT

We were wholly unable to come near you,
the dawning splendour of the light eternal,
and yet you came near to us
by that same free and innate goodness with which,
born from the Father's womb before the daystar,
you flashed out so wonderfully in the saints' first
   splendours.

   . . .

You were the great light
hidden in the bosom of your Father;
you came forth from your retreat into our market
   place.
You became a great lamp for the great,
and a small lamp for the little ones –
a lamp not only visible to our eyes
but palpable to our touch.

THE OVERFLOWING SPIRIT

Christ is common to all . . .
Why do you wish through spite to restrict Christ to
    a part?
Do you want the grace of the Spirit to be miserly?
Do you want his blessings restricted to you alone?
Allow the Spirit of the Lord to spread
and overflow
and pour itself out over all flesh
and fill the universe.
Do not imprison within the narrow limits of your
    heart
a generosity that is common to all.
The Spirit bestows his riches upon all,
and do you attempt to diminish the affluence of grace
and reduce its immensity to pettiness?
Christ scorns the miserly confines of an envious
    heart.
His goodness cannot be held back by your jealousy.
His goodness flows freely;
its oil pours itself not only into you
but also into neighbouring vessels.

THE GENEROSITY AND ABUNDANCE OF GOD

Truly we are not restricted in you, O Lord,
for you give profusely.
Nor do you give only to a few,
nor only a few gifts,
not in a parsimonious or niggardly way,
but anticipating our merits
and surpassing our desires.
No, in you we are not restricted
but we are restricted in our inmost affections.
Possessed of promises so great, my most beloved,
let us also extend ourselves;
let us extend ourselves to desire,
that we may be extended to receive.

GRATITUDE

Learn not to be tardy or sluggish in offering thanks
learn to offer thanks for each and every gift.
Take careful note, Scripture advises,
of what is set before you,
so that no gift of God,
great or moderate or small,
will be deprived of due thanksgiving.
We are even commended to gather up the fragments,
lest they be lost,
which means that we are not to forget even the
    smallest benefits.
Ingratitude is the soul's enemy,
a voiding of merits,
dissipation of the virtues,
wasting of benefits.
Ingratitude is a burning wind
that dries up the source of love,
the dew of mercy,
the streams of grace.

COMMENT

[p. 133] This section opens with this passage from Isaac of Stella which has appeared earlier in the book because I feel that it expresses so gently and lyrically what meditation on the Word, on Christ, meant to these twelfth-century Cistercians. I have included the Latin because, even if by now Latin usage is far less common, it does give a sense of the beauty of the original, and also to use the actual words as they were first written links us in some indefinable way with words used by countless unknown men and women down the centuries.

See chapter 2, note 17, p. 154.

[p. 134] The monk has come to the monastery to find God, and that must be his sole occupation. The seeking is sweet, but it is also a demanding labour and it asks the monk not to get preoccupied with other things – for the end goal is joy, perfect joy.

Jean Holman, 'Monastic joyfulness in Gilbert of Hoyland', CSQ 19 (1984.4), p. 325.

[p. 135] Gilbert of Hoyland then goes on to speak of how we are to treat the well and how we are to use faith, hope and love. 'Let faith clear your well, hope constantly dig deep into it, let love expand it.'

Holman, 'Monastic joyfulness', p. 325.

[p. 136] What Benedict wished for all his followers was a heart overflowing with love, and here Gilbert of Hoyland gives us a most lovely reflection on that same theme.

Holman, 'Monastic joyfulness', p. 334.

[p. 137] There was nothing that the early Cistercians liked more than to find in the Old Testaments signs and prefigurements of the truths and realities proclaimed in the New. This is a long, lyrical sermon on the cross in which Baldwin of Forde accompanies the Israelites on a journey which he sees as part of God's universal plan. As the Israelites 'passed over', marking their doorposts and lintels with the blood of a lamb, so too will we suffer, pass over and triumph with the sign of life – as did Christ the Lamb of God.

Sr Jane Patricia and David Bell, 'Two Sermons on Obedience and The Cross by Baldwin of Forde', CSQ 29 (1994.3), pp. 285–6.

[p. 138] John of Forde knows only too well the dangers of those who 'are so entirely given over to exterior concerns' that they can scarcely 'endure taking a deep breath in the depths of their souls or ever recollecting themselves'. Anyone called to serve brothers or sisters in a pastoral capacity must also look after themselves, and practise what they preach – which John sets out for his hearers in a very nicely chosen example.

Sermon 71; see Beverley Aitken, 'John of Forde, Twelfth-Century Guide for Twentieth-Century Monk' in Christopher Holdsworth and Hilary Costello (eds), *A Gathering of Friends: The Learning and Spirituality of John of Forde* (Kalamazoo, Mich.: CP, 1996), p. 193.

[p. 139] John of Forde is here giving good pastoral advice. Those who labour for the souls of others must also show concern for their own soul's health.

Sermon 57; see Aitken, 'John of Forde', p. 193.

[p. 140] In one of his sermons Gilbert of Hoyland compares the changed appearance of the soul with the transfiguration of the Lord on Mount Tabor. He says that we are transformed into the very image that we gaze on, so that by keeping our eyes fixed on Jesus as the guiding light of life we are transformed into a new creature. The biblical reference is from 2 Corinthians 3:18.

Holman, 'Monastic joyfulness', p. 331.

[p. 141] Here is good shadow, warm shadow, the shadow of the apple tree, full of healing power. Elsewhere John of Forde wrote, 'Here in this shadow you will find healing; here you will find real health in the reality that annihilates time; here you will gain power and strength.' Of course the shadow can be dark, the shadow of death. But, somehow the cross of Jesus, symbol of death, has become the symbol of life. Then by a further development of the symbolism, the cross made of wood becomes the tree that is fruitful, and because the apple tree is exceptionally fruitful it is the apple tree that symbolises Christ as Redeemer. After that, by only a small step, the followers of Christ are depicted as those who sit in the shadow of the apple tree.

Hilary Costello, 'Shade of Christ's Shade: Shadow Symbolism in John of Forde', CSQ 31 (1996.3), p. 265.

[p. 142] In his own times of greatest need Gilbert of Hoyland recalls the passion of Christ. Indeed the thought of the passion is never far from his mind, and he reminds us of it vividly and immediately as in these few words.

Holman, 'Monastic joyfulness', p. 329.

[p. 143] Here is a prayer to be delivered from the sad feelings, the boredom, depression and bitterness that Gilbert of Hoyland clearly knows only too well. Living in the north of England he must also have known the north wind – indeed he once used the phrase 'the horror of the north wind' to denote everything that was 'grievous, burdensome and oppressive' while the south denoted everything 'joyful and agreeable'. Elsewhere he said 'My south wind is my Christ. Let him blow through my garden.'

Holman, 'Monastic joyfulness', p. 328.

[p. 144] Here is Bernard of Clairvaux at his most gentle and encouraging. We need to let God's hope and joy and comfort enter into the grey and guilty areas of our life, so that we may be brought into happiness again.

Michael Casey, *The Art of Sacred Reading* (Australia, HarperCollins Dove, 1995), p. 72.

[p. 145] This sermon by Baldwin of Forde is a paean of praise, a celebration, a litany of thanksgiving for the cross. This section comes quite early on in the sermon, which opens with this list of resounding epithets which may be applied to the cross and which summarise its power and its purpose. It is, as its editors say, a masterpiece of rhetoric. We know that it was written for the canons of Waltham whose priory had been founded in the reign of King Canute to house a miraculous crucifix, carved in black marble. The house was refounded in 1177 and given to canons regular of the Augustinian order and clearly this work was composed by Baldwin for celebrations associated with that transfer.

I owe this to the article by Sr Jane Patricia and David Bell, CSQ 29.3 (1994), pp. 271–90.

[p. 146] Here is the evangelical charity, the love for others, the new commandment of the Lord, which the Cistercians put at the heart of their life. If I try to do the same, then each day can bring 'the dawn of fresh love'.

This comes from John of Forde and is taken from an article by Thomas Davis, 'Cistercian communio', CSQ 29 (1994.3), p. 32.

[p. 147] Aelred is here showing us the interaction among the three loves, the alternation of the three according to the variable disposition of each person and to the circumstances of life. Although there is an evident distinction in this triple love, a marvellous bond nevertheless does exist among the three, so that each is found in all, and all in each.

Charles Dumont, 'Fraternal love in the monastic doctrine of Aelred of Rievaulx', CSQ 32 (1997.1), p. 31.

[p. 148] Aelred here writes about what his vocation as director of souls means to him: to pour himself out entirely and to give himself utterly for his brothers. His model is Christ who lived and died for others.

It is taken from *Oratio Pastoralis*, 7, but I have lost the reference to the place in which I saw it.

[p. 149] It is typical of Bernard to remind us that there are many different times and moods in our lives just as there are many differing vocations, and God accepts and supports all. Again, apart from the fact that I read this in something that Michael Casey wrote, I can give no further reference.

[p. 150] Bernard tells me about a God who not only walks alongside me on the journey, and talks to me about heaven, but also sings favourite psalms – a joyous thought in times when I am tired and finding the path difficult.

Paul Diemer, *Love without Measure* (London: DLT, 1990), p. 90.

[p. 151] Beatrice of Nazareth was a Cistercian nun who lived from 1200 to 1268, and little is known of her life, though she is undoubtedly one of the most interesting of religious women in the Low Countries in the thirteenth century. She opens her treatise *There are Seven Manners of Loving* with a description of the experience of God as a cycle of love: 'There are seven manners of loving that come down from the highest place and which return again to the summit from which they came.' God as love and God as Creator are essential to her theological thinking. She is well aware that although she seeks to comprehend and be with the Godhead who is totally present in all things, yet God is a powerful, omniscient, and omnipresent perfect Being and incomprehensibly beyond all things. On the one hand the human soul cannot comprehend God; on the other it must seek God, try to become like God and rest in the love of God. The extract is taken from the seventh and last 'Manner' in which, in a highly poetic passage, she gives words to God's power and incomprehensibility.

Else Marie Wiberg Pedersen, 'Image of God – Image of Mary – image of woman: On the theology and spirituality of Beatrice of Nazareth', CSQ 29 (1994.2), pp. 209–21.

[p. 152] Time and again the Cistercians use the image of light. This is taken from Guerric of Igny's first sermon for the feast of the Purification when it would be more than ever in their minds. But as each day began with Vigils in the dark of the night and moved towards dawn and the coming of day, so the movement from darkness to light was written into their daily lives.

Pauline Matarasso, *The Cistercian World: Monastic Writings in the Twelfth Century* (Harmondsworth: Penguin Books, 1993), pp. 133–5.

[p. 154] John of Forde warns us against making too many assertions about the mystery of the Trinity, the relationship of Father to Son before time began. We simply cannot begin to grasp what he calls 'the secret mystery of the divine generation' and there would be a real danger of losing reverence for the Trinity by getting tangled up with useless questions. And yet we should try to realise that from the beginning, before time, in the eternity that is God, the Father generated his Son who is totally equal to himself. Thus they are one Light, one Wisdom, one Truth, one Holiness.

Hilary Costello, 'Secretarius Dominici pectoris: St John's Gospel in John of Forde' in Costello and Holdsworth (eds), *A Gathering of Friends*, p. 97.

[p. 155] Here is the summons to total generosity in all the recesses of the human heart. It is not sufficient for a person just to open the heart to Christ without being open to others as well.

Gilbert of Hoyland, quoted by Davis, 'Cistercian Communio', p. 309.

[p. 156] God can never be contained in our own small jar, says Gilbert of Hoyland, he pours himself out to us to overflowing. The only restriction is within my own self, the smallness of my own desire, so this prayer is one for openness, that my capacity to receive may be measureless.

Holman, 'Monastic joyfulness', p. 334.

[p. 157] This is from Bernard and I have chosen it as a most fitting conclusion to this book.

Diemer, *Love without Measure*, p. 122.

NOTES, REFERENCES AND COMMENTS

The following abbreviations will be used:

CSQ: *Cistercian Studies Quarterly* (originally *Cistercian Studies*), *Bulletin of Monastic Spirituality*, currently edited by Fr Charles S. Cummings, Holy Trinity Abbey, Utah, USA. I have used this widely as a source for the most recent Cistercian scholarship, presented in a way that is both scholarly and readable. It has a worldwide circulation and is increasingly read by numbers of lay people.

CP: Cistercian Publications, Kalamazoo, Michigan, USA. This is the main source for modern editions of all Cistercian texts. A complete catalogue of all texts in translation and studies in early, medieval and modern monasticism is available, at no cost, from Cistercian Publications (distributor), St Joseph's Abbey, Spencer, Mass. 01562, USA.

NOTES

Introduction

1. M. Basil Pennington, *The Last of the Fathers: The Cistercian Fathers of the Twelfth Century: A Collection of Essays* (Still River, Mass.: Still River Publications, 1983), p. x.
2. The quotation by Br Patrick Hart is taken from *Thomas Merton on St Bernard* (Kalamazoo, Mich.: CP, 1980), p. 6, and that by Jean Leclercq is from p. 19.
3. *Plant Dreaming Deep* (New York: W. W. Norton and Company, 1973), p. 124.

1. The Building

1. Charles Dumont, 'Contemplative action: Time in eternity according to St Bernard', CSQ 28 (1993.2), p. 156.
2. André Louf, *The Cistercian Way*, trans. Nivard Kinsella, monk of St Joseph Abbey, Roscrea, Ireland (Kalamazoo, Mich.: CP, 1989), p. 57.
3. *The Sign of Jonas* was originally published in 1953 by Harcourt,

Brace & Co., New York, and the quotations that I use here are taken from entries for 27 January and 28 December 1947.

4. Emero Stiegman, 'Analogues of the Cistercian abbey church' in Andrew Macleish (ed.), *The Medieval Monastery*, Medieval Studies at Minnesota 2 (n.d.), p. 20.

5. Pauline Matarasso, *The Cistercian World: Monastic Writings of the Twelfth Century* (Harmondsworth: Penguin Books, 1993), p. 154.

6. All this information about South Africa is taken from A. L. Balling, *Abbot Francis Pfanner, A Missionary Who Made History*, trans. Hugo Young (Marianhill Missionary Society, 1980), pp. 51–4.

7. Full text in Matarasso, *Cistercian World*, pp. 287–92.

8. *Silence in Heaven: A Book of the Monastic Life*, text by Thomas Merton, with ninety photographs, was published by Thames and Hudson in 1955 and gives a romantic picture of the Cistercian life of that period which retains a nostalgic appeal for many people.

2. Charism

1. Pauline Matarasso, *The Cistercian World: Monastic Writings in the Twelfth Century* (Harmondsworth: Penguin Books, 1993), p. 153.

2. The historical controversy which surrounds this is well dealt with by Pauline Matarasso on the first page of her *Cistercian World* where she says that these earliest texts emanating from Cîteaux are riddled with as many problems as a colander has holes.

3. Matarasso, *Cistercian World*, pp. 5–6.

4. How new was Cîteaux? This has been the source of happy or not so happy academic discussion for decades, debated in a plethora of learned journals, and I do not intend to contribute to a debate which Professor Christopher Holdsworth, another leading expert in the field of Cistercian studies, has called 'as bottomless and depressing a pit as the Slough of Despond'.

5. André Louf, *The Cistercian Way* (Kalamazoo, Mich.: CP, 1989), pp. 60–1.

6. R. W. Southern, *Western Society and the Church in the Middle Ages*, (Harmondsworth: Penguin Books, 1970), p. 255.

7. Thomas Merton, 'Saint Aelred of Rievaulx and the Cistercians', CSQ 23 (1988.1), p. 49.

8. Matarasso, *Cistercian World*, p. 7.

9. Pauline Matarasso includes eight such stories in her invaluable anthology. See *Cistercian World*, p. 297.

10. For a fascinating discussion of Cistercian practical skills see an article by Francis Evans (who, as a professor of engineering, can appreciate their technological expertise from a professional point of view), 'The engineer monks' in Ron Shoesmith and Ruth Richardson (eds), *A Definitive History of Dore Abbey* (Hereford: Logaston Press, 1997), pp. 139–48.

11. Thomas Merton, 'St Aelred of Rievaulx', CSQ 20 (1985.3), p. 214.
12. Jean Holman,'Monastic joyfulness in Gilbert of Hoyland', CSQ 19 (1984.4), p. 333. Sr Jean Holman was first a member of the Cistercian community of Stapehill in Dorset, which was founded in 1802 by a small group of refugee nuns from France. She is currently at Ubexy in France where she is working on Gilbert of Hoyland. I owe all that I know of him to her, and I shall be referring frequently to the material which this article has made available.
13. Matarasso, *Cistercian World*, p. 156.
14. This is taken from the notes of lectures given to the novices at Gethsemani by Thomas Merton which I was privileged to see when I was staying at the Abbey of New Clairvaux, Vina, California, a daughter house of Gethsemani.
15. I owe this to an article by Gaetano Raciti, 'The preferential option for the weak in the Aelredian community model', CSQ 32 (1997.1), pp. 16–17.
16. Chrysogonus Waddell has written a most useful piece on 'The place and meaning of the Work of God', CSQ 23 (1988.1), pp. 25–45.
17. M. Basil Pennington in *The Last of the Fathers: The Cistercian Fathers of the Twelfth Century* (Still River, Mass.: Still River Publications, 1983) gives this in Latin on p. 37 and translated on p. 45. The first word of each line in Latin opens *ipse, ipsum, ipso,* and *ipse* again for the seven final lines, a conceit which of course gets lost in translation. See above, p. 133, for the Latin text.
18. Holman, 'Monastic joyfulness', pp. 323–4.
19. Merton, 'St Aelred of Rievaulx', pp. 218–19.
20. M. Basil Pennington, *The Cistercians* (Collegeville, Minn.: The Liturgical Press, 1992), pp. 77–8.
21. Henri Nouwen, *The Genesee Diary* (New York: Image Books, 1981, and (London: DLT, 1995), p. 212.
22. The fact that the two articles I used for this section were written by an American Roman Catholic Cistercian nun and an English Anglican Benedictine monk, in itself makes a nice comment! Martha Driscoll, 'Blessed Maria Gabriella Sagheddu: A contemplative apostle of unity', CSQ 18 (1983.1), pp. 76–81, and Wilfred Weston, 'Blessed Maria Gabriella Sagheddu: patron of unity', CSQ 18 (1983.4), pp. 348–53. Sr Martha is now a member of the Cistercian monastery of Vitorchiano, which was formerly at Grottaferrata, where Sr Gabriella lived and died.
23. Shoesmith and Richardson (eds), *Dore Abbey*, p. 210.
24. For a short scholarly account of this, the earliest surviving Cistercian figure-painting in England, see Gillian Elias, 'The Cistercian Crucifixion at Forde Abbey Dorset, an artist's view', *Hallel* 21.1 (1996), pp. 55–60.
25. Most of Aelred's forty-five sermons have not appeared in English, but this, sermon 45 for the feast of the Assumption, has recently been

translated by Athanasius Sulavik, and published in CSQ 32 (1997.1), p. 124. In an introductory note Sr Catherine of Siena Priory, New York, comments on how pastoral these sermons are in tone and content.

26. Here I must record my gratitude for an article which I have found very illuminating: Marie Anne Mayeski, 'The Assumption as a monastic celebration: Aelred of Rievaulx's homilies for the feast', CSQ 29 (1994.4), pp. 395–411.

3. The Word

1. Henri Nouwen, *Genesee Diary* (New York: Image Books, 1981 and London: DLT, 1995), p. 100.

2. Michael Casey has written on this in 'The prayer of psalmody', CSQ 18 (1983.2), p. 109.

3. 'The psalms as prayer' in William O. Paulsell (ed.), *Sermons in a Monastery: Chapter Talks by Matthew Kelty* (Kalamazoo, Mich.: CP, 1983), pp. 9–14.

4. M. Basil Pennington, *The Cistercians* (Collegeville, Minn.: The Liturgical Press, 1992), p. 44.

5. I found the word 'attuned' in notes that I read at New Clairvaux, Vina, from Merton's talks to the novices. He wrote a short pamphlet, *Praying the Psalms* (Collegeville, Minn.: The Liturgical Press, 1956), which was published in England as *The Psalms are our Prayer* (London: Burns & Oates, 1957).

6. Chrysogonus Waddell, 'The place and meaning of the work of God in twelfth-century Cistercian life', CSQ 23 (1988.1), p. 31.

7. Bernard McGinn, *The Growth of Mysticism: From Gregory the Great to the Twelfth Century* (London: SCM Press, 1994), p. 176.

8. Pauline Matarasso, *The Cistercian World: Monastic Writings of the Twelfth Century* (Harmondsworth: Penguin Books, 1993), pp. 227–8.

9. Quoted from Walter Daniel's life of Aelred, Matarasso, *Cistercian World*, p. 161.

10. This is discussed by Renee H. Bennett in, 'The Song of Wisdom in Bernard's *Sermones Super Cantica Canticorum*', CSQ 30 (1995.2), pp. 147–79.

11. Sermon 5, trans. Athanasius Sulavik OP, 'Sermons on the feasts of Saint Mary', CSQ 32 (1997.1), p. 39.

12. Lawrence Braceland, 'The honeycomb in Gilbert of Hoyland', CSQ 17 (1982.3), p. 234.

13. Christopher Holdsworth, 'Two commentaries on the Song of Songs' in Christopher Holdsworth and Hilary Costello (eds), *A Gathering of Friends: The Learning and Spirituality of John of Forde* (Kalamazoo, Mich.: CP, 1996), pp. 161–2.

14. The sermon is given in Matarasso, *Cistercian World*, pp. 135–8.

15. Sermon 20, trans. Sulavik, 'Sermons on the feast of Saint Mary', pp. 51–2.
16. M. Basil Pennington, *The Last of the Fathers: The Cistercian Fathers of the Twelfth Century* (Still River, Mass.: Still River Publications, 1983), where it is given in Latin on page 37 and in translation on page 46. See p. 133.
17. Matarasso, *Cistercian World*, p. 227.
18. André Louf, *The Cistercian Way* (Kalamazoo, Mich.: CP, 1989), p. 125.
19. Pennington, *The Cistercians*, p. 48.
20. Jean Holman, 'Monastic joyfulness in Gilbert of Hoyland', CSQ 19 (1984.4), p. 327.
21. Quoted by Michael Casey, *The Art of Sacred Reading* (Australia: HarperCollins Dove, 1995), p. 14. This is one of the best books available on *lectio divina*.
22. I have written only very briefly on *lectio* since it is a subject on which there are a number of excellent books. I have already mentioned that by Michael Casey, and the other which I have found particularly valuable is also by a monk, Martin Smith SSJE, *The Word Is Very Near You: A Guide to Praying with Scripture* (Cambridge, Mass.: Cowley Publications, 1980).
23. I owe this to the article quoted above by Chysogonus Waddell, p. 30.
24. Casey, *Sacred Reading*, p. 135, note 7.

4. Simplicity

1. Chrysogonus Waddell, 'The place and meaning of the Work of God in twelfth-century Cistercian life', CSQ 23 (1988.1), pp. 25–45.
2. *The Spirit of Simplicity, Characteristic of the Cistercian Order*, Official Report (Kentucky: Trappist, 1948), p. 50; 'St Bernard on interior simplicity' in *Thomas Merton on St Bernard* (Kalamazoo, Mich.: CP, 1980).
3. Merton quotes this in 'Aelred of Rievaulx', CSQ 20 (1985.3), p. 216.
4. Henri Nouwen, *Genesee Diary* (New York: Image Books, 1981; London: DLT, 1995), pp. 76–7, 147.
5. I have explored this in my book *A Seven Day Journey with Thomas Merton* (Guildford: Eagle, and Ann Arbor, Mich.: Servant Publications, 1992).
6. This is one of my favourite quotations from Merton, but I cannot remember where I found it.
7. Thomas Merton, *The Silent Life* (New York: Farrar, Strauss and Cuhady, 1957), pp. 25–6.
8. Christopher Holdsworth, 'The blessings of work: the Cistercian view' in D. Baker (ed.), *Sanctity and Secularity: the Church and the World*, Studies in Church History, 10 (1973), pp. 68–9.
9. Pauline Matarasso, *The Cistercian World: Monastic Writings of the Twelfth Century* (Harmondsworth: Penguin Books, 1993), p. 206.

10. André Louf, *The Cistercian Way* (Kalamazoo, Mich.: CP, 1989), pp. 114–15.
11. *The Spirit of Simplicity*, p. 31.
12. Thomas Merton, 'St Aelred of Rievaulx', CSQ 20 (1985.3), p. 216.
13. Nouwen, *Genesee Diary*, pp. 129–30, pp. 146–7.
14. Beverley Aitken, 'John of Forde, twelfth-century guide for twentieth-century monk' in C. Holdsworth and H. Costello (eds), *A Gathering of Friends: The Learning and Spirituality of John of Forde* (Kalamazoo, Mich.: CP, 1996), p. 192.
15. M. Basil Pennington, *The Cistercians* (Collegeville, Minn.: The Liturgical Press, 1992), pp. 51–2.
16. This comes from the section on silence in the chapter called 'Asceticism – an exercise in grace' in Louf, *Cistercian Way*, pp. 92–4.

5. Integration

1. Marsha Dutton, 'John of Forde's *De Vita Beati Wulfrici*, a model for Cistercian contemplative life' in Christopher Holdsworth and Hilary Costello (eds), *A Gathering of Friends* (Kalamazoo, Mich.: CP, 1996), pp. 72–3.
2. Dutton, 'John of Forde', p. 67.
3. He then went on to say, 'The restoration of the Church must surely depend on a new kind of monasticism.' 'Contemplative action: Time in eternity according to St Bernard', CSQ 28 (1993.2), p. 145.
4. *Thomas Merton on St Bernard* (Kalamazoo, Mich.: CP, 1980), p. 64 and p. 99, n. 121.
5. R. W. Southern, *Western Society and the Church in the Middle Ages* (Harmondsworth: Penguin Books, 1970), p. 111.
6. *Merton on St Bernard*, p. 51 and p. 94, n. 73.
7. This comes from the article by Marsha Dutton, quoted above, p. 73.
8. Sermon 20, trans. A. Sulavik, 'Sermons on the feast of Saint Mary', CSQ 32 (1997.1), pp. 51–2.
9. Sermon 21, trans. Sulavik, 'Sermons', p. 66.
10. From Charles Dumont, 'Contemplative action: Time in eternity according to St Bernard', CSQ 28 (1993.2), pp. 150–1.

6. Growth

1. *Woods, Shore, Desert: A Notebook, May 1968* (Santa Fe: Museum of New Mexico Press, 1982), p. 8.
2. I owe much of the material in this section to an unpublished work by Michael Casey, *The Spiritual Teaching of Bernard of Clairvaux: An Interpretation*, privately printed in 1983, which I read when I was in Australia, and which was lent to me by the Good Samaritan Sisters, whose life follows the Rule of St Benedict.

3. A phrase from Chrysogonus Waddell, 'The place and meaning of the Work of God', CSQ 23 (1988.1), p. 40.

4. Basil Pennington, 'Abbot William – Spiritual father of Saint Thierry', CSQ 13 (1978.2), pp. 152–66. The actual quotation is on page 157. The following paragraph owes much to what I read in this article and especially the sections on page 161.

5. Pennington, 'Abbot William', p. 161.

6. Jean Holman, 'Monastic joyfulness in Gilbert of Hoyland', CSQ 19 (1984.4), p. 332.

7. Michael Casey, 'St Bernard of Clairvaux: The story of the King's Son', CSQ 18 (1983:1), pp. 16–23. Successive numbers of *Cistercian Studies Quarterly* carry further stories. Each tells of the battle for the human soul with a slightly different emphasis, but with the same use of vignettes and images, virtues and vices personified, and dramatic scenes.

8. I owe this quotation and the one that follows to Michael Casey's unpublished work referred to earlier in this chapter.

9. *The Seven Storey Mountain* (New York: Harcourt, Brace and Company, 1948), pp. 379–80. A slightly abridged edition was published in the UK as *Elected Silence* (London: Hollis and Carter, 1949).

10. Bernard McGinn, *The Growth of Mysticism: From Gregory the Great to the Twelfth Century* (London: SCM, 1994), p. 176.

11. Jean Leclercq, 'The imitation of Christ and the sacraments in the teaching of St Bernard', CSQ 19 (1974.1), pp. 36–54.

12. Sermon 43 on the Song of Songs, quoted in André Louf, *The Cistercian Way* (Kalamazoo, Mich.: CP, 1989), p. 63.

13. Holman, 'Monastic joyfulness', pp. 323–4.

14. Holman, 'Monastic joyfulness', p. 324.

15. Sermon 20 on the Assumption, trans. A. Sulavik, 'Sermons on the feast of Saint Mary', CSQ 32 (1997.1), pp. 51–2.

7. Love and Knowledge

1. M. Basil Pennington, *The Cistercians* (Collegeville, Minn.: The Liturgical Press, 1992), pp. 17, 20.

2. CSQ 18 (1983.4), p. 262.

3. M. Basil Pennington, *The Last of the Fathers: The Cistercian Fathers of the Twelfth Century* (Still River, Mass.: Still River Publications, 1983), pp. 67–8.

4. André Louf, *The Cistercian Way* (Kalamazoo, Mich.: CP, 1989), p. 279.

5. Thomas Merton, *The Spirit of Simplicity, Characteristic of the Cistercian Order* (Kentucky: Trappist, 1948), p. 89.

6. Merton, *Spirit of Simplicity*, p. 107.

7. André Louf, 'Humility and obedience in monastic tradition', CSQ 18 (1983.4), pp. 276–8.

8. Thomas Davis, of the Abbey of New Clairvaux, at the conclusion of a

discussion paper written in 1994 for a General Chapter on the theme 'The Community: School of Charity'. Thomas Davis is the Abbot of New Clairvaux, Vina, N. California, a daughter house of Gethsemani. He is writing here on 'Cistercian communio' in CSQ 29 (1994.3), p. 328.

9. *Thomas Merton on St Bernard* (Kalamazoo, Mich.: CP, 1980), p. 166.

10. *Merton on St Bernard*, p. 231, n. 62.

11. This sentence comes as a footnote in the article by Davis quoted above, p. 320.

12. I owe most of what I say here to an article by Hilary Costello, 'Secretarius Dominici pectoris, Saint John's Gospel in John of Forde' in C. Holdsworth and H. Costello (eds), *A Gathering of Friends: The Learning and Spirituality of John of Forde* (Kalamazoo, Mich.: CP, 1996), pp. 100–2.

13. Gerald S. Twomey, 'St Bernard's doctrine of the human person as the image and likeness of God in Sermons 80–83 on the Song of Songs', CSQ 18 (1982.2), pp. 144–5.

14. *Merton on St Bernard*, p. 228, n. 6.

15. I owe this to Michael Casey.

16. The text is given in Latin, as Appendix 1 of Jean Leclercq, *The Love of Learning and the Desire for God*, trans. Catharine Misrahi (New York: Fordham University Press, 2nd edn 1974; London: SPCK, 1978).

17. Pauline Matarasso, *The Cistercian World: Monastic Writings of the Twelfth Century* (Harmondsworth: Penguin Books, 1993), p. 166.

8. The Sharing of Love

1. These words of Bernard follow on soon after those on p. 112.

2. M. Basil Pennington, *The Last of the Fathers: The Cistercian Fathers of the Twelfth Century* (Still River, Mass.: Still River Publications, 1992), p. 115.

3. Charles Dumont, 'Fraternal love in the monastic doctrine of Aelred of Rievaulx', CSQ 32 (1997.1), p. 33.

4. Thomas Merton, 'Saint Aelred of Rievaulx and the Cistercians', CSQ 23 (1988.1), p. 52.

5. André Louf, *The Cistercian Way* (Kalamazoo, Mich.: CP, 1989), p. 30.

6. Pennington, *Last of the Fathers*, p. 198.

7. Beverley Aitken discusses this and much more that is illuminating about John of Forde in her chapter in C. Holdsworth and H. Costello (eds), *A Gathering of Friends: The Learning and Spirituality of John of Forde* (Kalamazoo, Mich.: CP, 1996), pp. 189–98.

8. Aitken in *A Gathering of Friends*, p. 197.

9. Quoted in Pauline Matarasso, *The Cistercian World: Monastic Writings of the Twelfth Century* (Harmondsworth: Penguin Books, 1993), p. 218.

10. I owe this to Thomas Davis, 'Cistercian communio', CSQ 29 (1994.3), p. 325.
11. Louf, *Cistercian Way*, p. 128.
12. Quoted in Matarasso, *Cistercian World*, p. 184.
13. Matarasso, *Cistercian World*, p. 159.

9. Portrait Gallery

I owe a great deal of what I say here to the excellent short introductions given by Pauline Matarasso in her most useful anthology *The Cistercian World: Monastic Writings in the Twelfth Century* (Harmondsworth: Penguin Books, 1993), which has been such an enormous help in the writing of this book, and which I most warmly recommend to anyone wishing to read further in the original twelfth-century monastic texts.

10. *Lectio*

1. Comment on the passages given here follows on p. 145. The immediate source of each passage, if known, is given at the end of the comment.